The Lazy Dog Way

HOW TO BUILD YOUR BUSINESS, BRAND, AND LIFE PUTTING PEOPLE FIRST

From the author of
Millionaire in Flip Flops

Sue Cooper

ISBN-13 – 978-0-9860308-7-1
ISBN 10 – 0-9860308-7-2

Managing Editor: Katie Elzer-Peters
Development Editor: Billie Brownell
Design: Nathan Bauer

Front photo by Jessica Robb at
https://jessicamrobb.zenfolio.com
Back photo courtesy of Lazy Dog

For more information visit www.MillionaireInFlipFlops.com
Printed in the United States of America.

Dedication

To my mom and dad, the true entrepreneur, business, and life role models who lead by example and showed me how to create a living and a life by taking care of myself, working hard, having experiences, having fun, traveling the world, keeping a positive attitude, just doing it, leading with kindness, and sharing with others.

TABLE OF CONTENTS

THE FISHERMAN

An American tourist was at the pier of a small coastal Mexican village when a small boat with only one fisherman aboard docked. Inside the small boat were several large yellowfin tuna. The tourist complimented the fisherman on the quality of his fish and asked how long it took to catch them.

The fisherman replied, "Only a little while."

The tourist then asked, "Why didn't you stay out longer and catch more fish?"

The fisherman said, "With this, I have more than enough to support my family's needs."

The tourist then asked, "But what do you do with the rest of your time?"

The fisherman said, "I sleep late, fish a little, play with my children, take a siesta with my wife, Maria, stroll into the village each evening where I sip wine, and play guitar with my amigos. I have a full and busy life."

The tourist scoffed, "I can help you. You should spend more time fishing, and with the proceeds, buy a bigger boat. With the proceeds from the bigger boat, you could buy several boats. Eventually, you would have a fleet of fishing boats. Instead of selling your catch to a middleman, you would sell directly to the processor, eventually opening your own cannery. You would control the product, processing, and distribution. You could leave this small coastal fishing village and move to Mexico City, then Los Angeles, and eventually, New York, where you could run your ever-expanding enterprise."

The fisherman asked, "But how long will this all take?"

The tourist replied, "Fifteen to 20 years."

"But what then?" asked the fisherman.

The tourist laughed and said, "That's the best part. When the time is right, you would sell your company stock to the public and become very rich. You would make millions."

"Millions? Then what?"

The tourist said, "Then, you would retire. Move to a small coastal fishing village where you would sleep late, fish a little, play with your kids, take siestas with your wife, stroll to the village in the evenings where you could sip wine, and play your guitar with your amigos."

Introduction

What if you…
Quit your job
Moved to an island
Opened your own business
Hired your best friends
Rescued a dog
Traveled the world
And wrote a book about it?
Well, that's my story.

WELCOME TO LAZY DOG ADVENTURES

When I was younger, I had big dreams. Building a business, traveling the world, running marathons, writing a book, earning enough money to do everything I wanted, making a difference, living on an island, rescuing dogs, having crazy adventures, and living a life full of experiences were all in my plan. Things turned out better than I ever dreamt because there was one thing I forgot to put in my dreams: people. It was in focusing on people that I built my business, brand, and my life even better than I could have imagined.

Building up people, bringing the energy to people, listening to people, caring about people, including yourself — these things are the backbone of building a successful business, a brand, and a life.

I've always run my business the way I live my life. You know that famous quote, "The way you do anything is the way you do everything"? Well, I'm passionate about business, and my philosophies on how to build a successful company not only apply to business but also to my personal life, my relationships, my fitness, my health, how I travel, and how I move through life. Much of what you read in this book can be applied to many areas of your life.

I have always had business in my blood. My dad was the youngest director at IBM at the age of 34, and my mom was an entrepreneur, turning her hobby into a home business in our basement. I wanted to work for a big company and dress up every day like my dad. My plan was to work for a big company, move up the ladder, work for them for 30 years, and then retire. So, I went to work for an international footwear company called H. H. Brown.

I was hired as an entry level employee in customer service, but I didn't want to be in that role. I would come in early and stay late, doing my customer service job during my 8 hours and assisting anyone else in other departments who came in early and stayed late. I learned so much "after hours." Sometimes, it would mean going to dinner or having drinks with people who also worked late. I was on the "inside," hanging with the divisional president and marketing director. I helped any way I could. I particularly liked spending time with Craig, the marketing director. I wanted to be in marketing, not in customer service. One day, Craig and I were talking, and he asked me if I could do anything for the company, what I would do. I said that if I could create my own job in the company, I would be a "tech rep." I would travel around the country to our best accounts and teach the employees of those stores all the "technical" details, stories, and selling points so that they could sell more of our shoes. The more connected someone is with a product, the easier it is to sell. I wanted to be based out of the headquarters office, assist sales reps, handle marketing, and make my own travel schedule. I also said, "Oh, and you will see my positive results from the increase in sales from each store I visit." Craig was on-board, and I just created my own job doing all the things I wanted by being able to quantify my results in increased sales for the company.

"If it doesn't exist, create it."

This motto has been the backbone of all I do, and it will come up in almost every aspect of this book. Don't ever settle for what you know. There's so much in this world that we don't even know exists. If what you are looking for doesn't exist, create it.

For the next couple of years, I was the first tech rep of the marketing department. It was Craig and me. But as corporate goes, so go the great ones. Craig "left," as did some of the best people in the company. But they never hired replacements, so I jumped in wherever I was needed and took on more and more responsibility. I slowly earned more money, but what mattered most to me was that that I was learning how to do things and lots of how *not* to do things.

After a few years, I was invited to the executive conference, a two-day event for all nine of our worldwide divisions. I wasn't an executive, but they asked me to come anyway. I was intimidated and in way over my head at the event. I just took it all in, listened, and learned some more. At the formal dinner one night, awards were handed out to the Executive of the Year in each division. Yes, that ended up being me. Voted on by my peers, everyone in the office voted for me, even though I wasn't an executive. I guess I was now.

I was over the moon. I was on my way. I was an executive. I celebrated that night with my company, and when I woke up in the hotel room the next morning, I was the saddest I had ever been. Why? Because the rest of my life was in shambles. I loved my job, and I loved business, but it hit me that not one thing can make you happy. My relationship was suffering, I was traveling all the time and so, wasn't around to play with my friends, I was getting out of shape from all the days traveling, I couldn't get a dog because I wasn't around much, and I wasn't too keen on the "corporate" way of doing business. That's when I realized that success, and by *success* I mean feeling fulfilled and happy, wasn't about the job title and money—it was about doing what I love, living where I love, surrounded by people I love, every day.

So, I quit! But I didn't quit because I wanted to "drop out." I was actually looking to jump in.

I realized that if I had to work in this life, and this, by the way, is a shout out to all of you reading this book because there is only a small percentage of people who don't have to work in this life, that I wanted to enjoy what I do, the life I live, and the people who are in it, **every day.**

When I told my parents, whom I greatly admire, that I was quitting my job, they were disappointed. They told me that I was choosing a difficult path but that they loved me and would support me. This was the best thing my parents could have done for me—letting me go but supporting me even when they didn't agree with what I was doing.

———

"Success doesn't make you fulfilled; fulfillment makes you successful."

———

I always had a dream of living on an island and opening my own business, though I never knew what kind of business. I had no idea what exactly I wanted to do, but I did have what I like to call a "Personal Culture."

My Personal Culture

I knew I didn't like the politics of corporate life, but I loved business. I wanted to live on an island, have a dog, and bring my dog to work. I wanted to create an atmosphere where I wanted to come to work, where I could hire my friends, and *they* would want to come to work. I wanted to work outside, work with lots of outside companies, build a brand, educate, share, create. I wanted to empower people to "do things," make a difference, and have unlimited growth potential.

Having a personal culture gave my life more focus. I knew what I wanted and what I didn't want.

I packed up a moving truck, got rid of my brand-new car, and moved to the island of Key West, the warmest place on the map in the US.

I didn't know exactly what I wanted to do for business, so I started saying "yes" to everything. Saying "yes" is a lifestyle philosophy for me personally and at work. Saying "yes" can get you unstuck and, most importantly, open your world up to all the things and people you have no idea even exist. More great things come from saying yes than saying no.

The SCoop

Saying "yes" always leads to more fun.

I loved being on the water, so I would go out on kayak tours with a company called Mosquito Coast. I went out with them so much, they offered me a job. I started working as a kayak guide. Shortly after I started working as a guide, the owner decided he was going to pursue his love of wine. He said he would like me to buy the business; otherwise, he would close the doors. He made me an offer I couldn't refuse, which led me to owning my first business, a kayak tour business. Over 20 years later, I have expanded into tours, rentals, events, classes, workshops, and merchandise, all the while doing what I love to do, building a brand, and creating experiences that make a difference in people's lives, every day. I am living my personal culture from all those years ago.

The best part is that I don't have to be at work (thanks to my amazing staff), but I actually love being at work. I'm constantly learning every day. My work is an extension of my lifestyle. My staff are some of my best friends. Every year, about 28,000 people enjoy adventures with Lazy Dog, and it's so fun meeting new people and creating an opportunity for them to go out and have a memorable experience, to be "the highlight of their vacation" or to put on an event where someone says, "I never thought I could do that." Making a difference in peoples' lives through a paddle excursion, paddle race, seminar, workshop, book, or simply by having an experience and sharing it—this is what drives me. I feel so much gratitude that my job allows me the opportunity to make a difference in someone's life. You could look at it as just a job, but imagine someone working hard all year, saving their money and coming to Key West for a vacation, and then, they choose a Lazy Dog adventure. We have the honor of being part of their experience and to make it so remarkable that they will remember it forever. We get to do this daily, and we have the utmost gratitude.

"If it were easy, everyone would be doing it."

I can't tell you how many times I've heard this: "I'd love to do what you do." Well, you can, my friend. It simply means you will have to give up some things, make sacrifices, and make big changes— but anything worthwhile will make you do all that. Whether in business or life, if it were easy, everyone would be doing it.

The philosophies that I have learned over the years through Lazy Dog and my early years in the Cooper household have formed what I now call "The Lazy Dog Way." Whether at work, play, or anywhere else, the way I do anything is the way I do everything. Sue at work is also Sue at play. Work and life are not balanced; they are integrated. That is how you make a great life for yourself. By doing something you are passionate about, every day.

In this book, I want to share with you the way we do business and life at Lazy Dog. The way I like to do that is through stories, a checklist of how-to, a why, which is always important, and in action plans. The action plans are important to me because, looking back, I can see that it was answering questions that led me to taking action, which led me to this remarkable life. For this, I thank my sister, Julie, and Tony Robbins' 30-day motivational cassette tapes.

"Action trumps knowledge."

I remember several years ago being in my car and listening to Tony Robbins 30-day Change Your Life cassette tapes. I was blasting through them because I didn't want to be sad. I was doing 1 to 3 tapes a day. While in my car, I'd hear Tony say something like, "You are probably driving while listening to this tape. You are looking for something; that's why you are listening. You're probably sad, slouched over, breathing shallowly, not smiling. I want you to sit up right with good posture, put a smile on your face, take deep breaths, and think of something that makes you happy." I did all this, and for a brief moment, I felt great. That's when it hit me. The only person who can change things for me is me. I can choose to sit and wallow, or I can choose not to. I could change my emotional state by changing my physical state. I had the power. I chose to be happy, to make things happen, to take chances, and to be the best version of myself. No one was going to do it for me, not even Tony. Tony merely showed me the path. We each have a choice, so choose happiness because the alternative stinks.

In 2018, I was lucky enough to meet Tony Robbins. I walked up to him, gave him a giant bear hug, and said, "Thank you. You saved my life." Tony responded by saying, "No, Sue, you did." You know what, yes, I did. It's up to you what you want to do with your life (though I suggest doing everything you can). We only have one life—what are you going to do with yours?

I don't want to get too off-track because this is a business book, but my life is an extension of my business. My voice is also Lazy Dog's voice. My vision, beliefs, and values are also those of Lazy Dog. What I share with you in this "business" book can also be used in life, in relationships, and in how you care for yourself.

Simply because you find your path, do what you love, live where you want, and surround yourself with people whom you love doesn't mean life is easy, but life *is* much easier to handle when you are doing what you love, with those you love, and living where you love.

I've heard people say I make running a business look easy. On the one hand, it is because I keep it simple, don't overcomplicate things, and love what I do. Most importantly, I keep the focus on the most important part of any successful company, the people. I work hard and enjoy what I do; it's my way of life. You will increase your chances of success if you love what you do. I try to be a minimalist: no big office, no warehouse, no mounds of paperwork. At Lazy Dog, we keep things simple so that we can focus on our jobs, which is being remarkable at what we do so that people can have a memorable experience. Experiences make us who we are, and we want to be part of that.

"Life isn't about making a living; it's about making a life."

I remember driving down the Keys and reading a billboard that said, "Escape your everyday life." I thought, why would I want to do that? I do what I love, with people that I love, live where I love, *and* I have a dog. These are all things that we can create. Hopefully, this book will help you in such a way that you don't feel you need to escape your everyday life.

As you read this book, I highly recommend you work the action plans and, more specifically, write your answers down. There is power in writing things down. Remember, thinking about something doesn't make it happen. Applying your answers and your plan and taking action will make things happen. You can use these action plans and philosophies specifically for business but, also, for your own life.

———

"Find your passion and make it your life's work."

———

I believe that our ultimate purpose in this life is to grow, give back, and make a difference. I hope this book will help you find your passion, your purpose, and make it your life's work, every day.

I'm not merely a business owner, I'm an entrepreneur. There's a difference. An entrepreneur is a way of life; there is no end goal because there will always be another goal or challenge. You won't find me sitting by the pool on vacation. I thrive on the journey and celebrate in the destination, then move on to the next journey. I love experiencing as much as possible in all I do. I want to live and experience this life; it doesn't matter if I'm good at what I do, it only matters that I do it and that I learn and grow from every experience and have fun. Then, of course, that I share with others. It's not going to happen unless you make it happen, I'm simply here to get you moving, give you some ideas, ask the tough questions, and get you thinking about the everyday a little differently. A different approach to the same old situation. That's all it takes.

Whatever you do for work, it's important that you love what you do because you will be spending one-third of your life doing it. Our motto at Lazy Dog has always been, "Find your passion and make it your life's work." But there is a fine line between following your passion and making money. Find something you love that can make you money.

The SCoop

The secrets to success.

The Outside: Other People

I've always had big dreams, including work, fitness, wealth…but the one thing I realize now that I never considered was the role of people in my life. It's the people I'm surrounded by who have helped me exceed my dreams. In setting personal goals, people are somehow lost in the "dream big," but life is always more exciting with fun, loving people by your side. If you're only going to do one thing after reading this book, value the great people in your life and keep adding more of them. Our overall fulfillment in all we do is directly related to our personal connections.

The Inside Job: Ourselves

For many of us who have attempted to change the outward workings of the people in our lives, change doesn't come from the outside, it comes from the inside. We waste a lot of time trying to change the outside world when all we need to do is the inner work. By changing how we look at things, finding our why, doing what we love, and changing our responses, we can completely revamp our lives, business/work, relationships, and health.

When I'm asked what I attribute my success to, I confidently say "my mindset." How? I changed the way I look at things, I changed my responses, I took 100% responsibility for things in my life, and I spent time doing the inner work, specifically with goal setting and action plans. Instead of looking outside at what existed and what didn't exist, I looked inward. I spent time on the "inside job" figuring out *who* I wanted to be and *why*. Then, I created goals with specific action plans to make it all happen. I took care of myself first so that I could have unlimited resources for others. Most importantly, I realized that every morning, I have a choice to be happy or not. I choose to be happy. Attitude is everything, and it can change absolutely everything.

Feel Your Way

When I first started my business, I was doing things the way I thought they should be done because nobody was there to tell me how to do anything. The internet was in its early stages; it was so slow, and it wasn't full of all the information that we have today. I couldn't simply Google a question and have an answer. Questions such as: How to start a business? How to market a company with limited funds? How to hire? How to set prices? How to build a customer base? The early years were about being consistent and not getting discouraged. I worked more off "feel" than information. I did things the way I felt I should, which was not always the way everyone else was doing them. Although that was much harder than it would be today, with so much information available on the internet, it benefited me because I was doing what worked for my company, all by myself and in Key West. I wasn't doing what everyone else was doing, which was good because I didn't want to be like everyone else. I wanted my company to stand out. In today's world, I think it's important to bring back that element of "feel" into the company and do things that organically work for you.

One of my favorite business people to follow is Sara Blakely, owner and creator of Spanx, the women's undergarment company, and the wife of my "life" coach, Jesse Itzler. One of my favorites of Sara's stories is when she "felt" her way through business and how she thought she should sell Spanx and not how everyone else did it. When Sara created Spanx, she called Neiman Marcus and asked to speak to the buyer. When she met with the buyer, Sara explained how her product could benefit the buyer's customers. Sara ended up getting an order for seven stores. After her appointment, some other people in the industry asked her how she did it. She said she just called and asked for a meeting. The response was, "Well, that's not how you do it. You invest in a booth at all the expos and shows, and after a couple years when the buyers see you're still around, they will give you the time." Sara didn't know how to do it, so she did it the way she felt she should. Now, her company is worth over $1 billion.

What This Book Is About

This is a business book, and so, to start, I am going to focus on the most important thing we can to put you on a path to success: *you*. We will start with your story, your happiness, and your relationships. After establishing the core in you, we will build from there to leadership, management, customer service, marketing, competition, and other business-specific topics.

Business is simple, but we tend to make it complex, as we do life. This book is about stripping away the complexities and looking at the core basics to building a successful business and life. I believe in work/life *integration*, the intertwining of work and life, not work/life balance, which is more of a separation of the two. It's about developing the best you can be, doing what you love, having more fun, doing it all, and being kind while building your business and life the way you want.

The person I am outside of work is the same person I am at work. It's when we put on other personas that don't match who we really are that things become difficult.

You are the factor in all aspects of the business. With that in mind, I have included what I think are the most important tools to help you find who you are and how you want to do it, with action plans.

Although this is a business book, many of the philosophies can be used in life too. The way you do anything is the way you do everything. If you are a procrastinator at work, you are probably a procrastinator at home. Apply the tools in this book to all aspects of your life.

It is imperative that you find what you love and are passionate about, and live it out. When you are doing what you are passionate about, three things happen: things become a lot easier because you are on the right path, daily opportunities begin to present themselves, and opportunities you never knew existed become real possibilities. *That's* where life gets fun.

I'll start you off with one of my DO THIS action plans. The DO THIS sections are the most important parts of the book because they take you one step further than merely thinking about change. If you want to make some changes in your life, DO THIS. Once you do, the action plans take action. Change doesn't come about from learning and knowing; it's about applying.

So—before we get too involved in the book, let's see where you are at.

 # DO THIS: WHAT'S YOUR STORY?

The story you tell yourself and to others can determine the state of your happiness. Your story, as told by you, is a good benchmark to find out where you are.

Action 1
If we were meeting for the first time and I asked you to tell me about yourself, what would you say? Write it down; you have 2 minutes. GO!

....

....

....

....

Action 2
If you were to rate this story from 1 to 10 (10 being remarkable and awesome), what rating would you give it? Oh, by the way, you can't use the number 7.

What's your rating?_____Answer before you continue on.

This is something I learned from Tim Ferris, and it works. Anytime you're asked to rate something from 1–10, take out the number 7; you'll have to choose either 6 or 8, which is a D or a B. That will make a big difference in your answer.

This story that you tell, has it changed over the years?

Do you continue to tell the same story?

Is this story exciting to you?

The story you tell yourself is what you believe about yourself and what others will believe about you.

Action 3

If you didn't rate your story as a 10, what is missing? Rewrite your story as a 10. Here's how to start. Your new story will be a remarkable story of your life. It may include but not be limited to the following ideas:

That one thing you've dreamed of your entire life…
Things that you are passionate about or bring you joy…
Your best qualities are…
*These great things **will** happen…*
This is what your impact on the world looks like…

Write your new story.

By taking action and rewriting your story, you move yourself out of the past and move toward the future you want. You also eliminate self-doubt and negative talk and replace it with encouragement and inspiration.

What's Holding You Back?

Through spending time with people in my workshops, there are two consistent "issues" that seem to come up: negative self-talk/self-doubt and not enough time.

When I met Sara Blakely, she said one of the things that holds her back is negative self-talk. What? If she has it, then *everyone* probably has it. So, how do we conquer negative self-talk? We become our thoughts, so by being aware of our thoughts and changing them, we can move past self-doubt. However, it's not that easy. It takes awareness, practice, and consistency. If we could get out of our own way, imagine the results. Knowing that is enough to make changes.

The other issue is not having enough time. The simple cure for this is to start saying "no" to anything that doesn't relate to your personal and professional goals. Eliminating the "other stuff" will help you prioritize the things you really want to do, and help you focus on and crush your goals.

"Action trumps knowledge."

DO THIS:
Make a list of anything that is holding you back.

Then, come up with an action plan to push past what's holding you back.

Part One

You First

Chapter 1

YOU FIRST

*"Bring the 100% version of yourself to every day. No one
wants to be a B-version of themselves."*

Your success, happiness, and fulfillment from your work, personal
relationships, health, fitness, and everything else in between are all
dependent on one thing: you. That might seem scary, maybe even
lonely, but I want you to see it from a different viewpoint. I want
you to see how lucky and grateful you are that your life is up to
you. No one else, only you. This might not seem clear to you, with
other people, your job, responsibilities, bosses, and so forth in the
picture, but you have the power. You, the leader of you, hold the
key to your success.

The SCoop

If there's a secret to success, this is it...

The absolute first thing you must do, every day, is take care of
yourself. Some of you may say, "that's selfish"; some may say, "I
don't have the time." But here's the hard truth: if you don't take
care of yourself first, you will be putting a fraction of your best
self out there every day. That isn't fair to you, and it is definitely
shorting all that you do in work and personal relationships. So,
what were you saying about being selfish? Why would you want to
be an 80% version of yourself? Would you really feel good about
going through life with your B-game every day? Taking care of you
first will improve all aspects of your life.

Bringing my A game started back when I was young. From an early
age I always woke up well before the sunrise and went for a run.

Doing this has been a part of my life since I can remember. Taking this time for myself has given me not only the physical energy to bring to life every day but the mental energy, taking the time with my thoughts and clearing my mind. Running is also when I am the most creative and when I have come up with most of my best ideas. It's when we take time for ourselves that clarity arrives. It's hard to know how to figure things out when we are constantly on the go. I truly believe that it is this time, the first few hours of each day, that have greatly led to my success in all I do.

The SCoop

Doing the mind work will lead to massive results in everything that you do.

"You have to change the way you think before you can change your life."

There have been many studies and reports on the practices and traits of some of the most "successful" people in the world (such as Richard Branson and Oprah), and almost everyone will say that these people take a minimum of 2 hours a day for self-care, working on their body and their minds.

I'm a big believer in doing the mind work. Mind work is a game changer. Just ask Michael Jordan, Tom Brady, and LeBron James. They see the advantages of doing the mind work to better their physical game. But what if we did the mind work to better our game: our life, work, relationships? Think about the benefits. The mind work with the body work can catapult your life in all areas.

"The mental (work) is what separates the good players from the great players." Michael Jordan

Imagine if we worked our minds out the way we work our body out. Do the inner work, and you will see massive growth. Why not give it a try? What's the worst that can happen, you end up more fulfilled and happier? By doing the inner work, your "outside" world will boom. Your work, play, fitness, and relationships will all benefit. No more looking to change other people and things; this is about you.

"Whatever you want to do you will do better if you are fit."

Two Life Game Changers to Get You Started

Exercise. One of the best ways to take care of yourself is to exercise. Exercise is the most important habit you can develop to grow and transform your business and life—really, all areas of your life. It brings confidence, energy, mental sharpness, and the ability to be more productive and manage stress, among other things. Through exercise, you can clear through the clutter in your mind to see what you need and want and to give yourself some direction.

Mind Work. Have you ever paid attention to the thoughts and information that you put into you mind every day? Thoughts we put in our mind are just like what we feed our body. These thoughts fuel our body. When we put "junk" thoughts in our mind, it fuels our mind with junk, and you're not going to be living the 100% version of yourself with junk. You are making things much harder on yourself. Yes, that's right, *you* are doing it to yourself. So, stop getting in your own way; stop being your worst critic, and become your biggest fan.

What you listen to every day will determine what you think about. Listen to sappy love songs, you will feel sad. Listen to Tony Robbins' "Hour of Power," you will feel energized.

23

How do you talk to yourself? What are some common things you say to yourself every day?

_____

_____

_____

The average person has between 12,000 and 60,000 thoughts per day. Of those, 80% are negative, and 95% are the same thoughts as the day before. Simply changing your thoughts can greatly affect your life. So, how do we do that?

Awareness. Become aware of what you are feeding your mind. What thoughts and information are you feeding yourself every day?

Consistency. Once you become aware, it's time to change the thoughts as quickly as you can. In the beginning, this might be hard because your habit is to be negative and repetitive. Keep at it, and it gets easier. It's like training a muscle. Don't get discouraged.

Our mind doesn't know the difference between what's real and what you have made up in your head. Have you ever made yourself cry merely by thinking about something that hasn't even happened?

Words and phrases. Again, the mind doesn't know what's real, so be careful how you phrase things. By saying, "I hope I don't get sick," your mind and body hear "get sick." Instead, use positive words and phrases such as, "I want to stay healthy."

If you want to be great at what you do, anything you do, you need to be the best you 100% every day!

There are many people who don't want to get in their minds and find out why they do what they do, but for those willing, like yourselves, it can completely change your life for the better, in all areas of your life, *every day.*

If you're up for the challenge, at the end of this chapter, I have put together a mind/body daily routine that can catapult you into happier and healthier living in all you do: work, relationships, wellness, life. It's that easy.

———

"Successful, and by successful I mean happy and fulfilled, people put themselves first."

———

DO THIS:
Creating a Successful 8-before-8

Most successful/happy people have a morning routine that sets them up for a successful day. I have read about many successful people's morning routines. Some of the most popular routines include workouts, meditating, making the bed, and so forth. I decided to try some of these routines for myself. By adding and subtracting what other people did to my routine, I was eventually able to create my own. By establishing my own morning power routine, I was able to jump-start every day. You can too!

TIME TO TAKE ACTION
What's your morning routine? List 8 things you do in your current morning routine before 8 a.m. (or during the first two hours of your day).

1. _____

2. _____

3. _____

4. ....

5. ....

6. ....

7. ....

8. ....

After reviewing your list, do you see anything you want to add or delete from your current routine? Go ahead and make any changes you think may improve your day. This is your list; it's not based on anyone but you. Once you have finalized an update on your list, try it out. If there is something that doesn't work, adjust it until you have fine-tuned your successful start to every day. Also, keep notes to the side of each routine about how it makes you feel, and so on.

Having a successful morning routine can make you more productive, focused, energized, and effective. Who wouldn't want that?

Here's an example of my 8 before 8, what I do to bring my A game every day, how I start the day so that I can come out feeling energized.

1. Say "thank you." When I put my feet on the ground every morning, I say "thank you," starting the day with gratitude.
2. Look out window and take 3 deep breaths.
3. Drink warm water with a squeeze of lemon.
4. Sunrise walk with my dog and cup of tea.
5. Stretch and yoga exercises (5 minutes).
6. Run.
7. Listen to a podcast (usually while running), something

new to feed my mind every morning).
8. Meditate.

Notice that looking at my phone isn't on the list. I do this after my 8. Looking at your phone first thing starts you off reacting to things and people rather than being proactive in your day.

Inside Job

Doing the inner work, taking the time for your mind and body, will not only help you become more productive; it will improve all areas of your life: work, relationships, and wellness. Changing the way you look at things, at how things are done, can change everything. So, if you want a different result, you need to look inside and change how you look at things. Change your response; a different response will lead to a different outcome. This simple adjustment has been a lifesaver for me. Honestly, it changed everything for me. I began noticing the things that didn't work for me and for the business and changed up my responses as necessary. I stopped wasting time doing the same thing and reacting the same way.

If I could share with you the most important part of your overall success in life, it will be your attitude. Attitude really is everything. You will improve your happiness and level of success with a better attitude. People will enjoy spending time with you and helping you if you have a good attitude. Bring it every day, and you will see massive growth.

Growing takes constant work, a job that is never done. Growing also creates progress, and progress leads to happiness. If you don't grow, you will most likely find yourself settling, and settling typically doesn't feel so good. Keep moving, shaking, doing, experiencing, learning, and, most importantly, *apply* it all. When you reach your goals, make new ones or edit as you go. Never stop growing.

You First Mind/Body "Workout"

It's so simple, why wouldn't we do it?

Increasing health, well-being, intelligence, and productivity is so easy that we just don't do it. But you know who does do it? Michael Jordan, Tom Brady, Oprah Winfrey, Lebron James, and Will Smith.

Do what, you ask? Train the mind. They do the mind work.

There are so many things, simple things, we can do in our day that can be game changers to our happiness and success in our work, relationships, and life. We all know what they are, and we think we will do them, but then, because they are so easy, we keep pushing them aside, year after year.

What if I told you that if you drink water, get a good night's sleep, take deep breaths, visualize, meditate, take a nap, and brush and floss your teeth, that you would:
- Feel more energized?
- Feel motivated?
- Feel less stress, fatigue, anxiety, and depression?
- Decrease your blood pressure?
- Boost your mood?
- Improve your memory, creativity, and productivity?
- Lose weight?
- And, on top of all that, live longer?

Would you do it? Most would say "yes?" But then, why don't we? Is it that we are too busy doing things that negatively affect our overall wellness that we don't have the time to do the things that can improve our health and happiness?

We are all probably doing these things; however, we just aren't doing them enough that they benefit us. For example, if you are drinking a couple glasses of water a day, great, but drinking only a couple glasses means you're in deficit. You are not hydrated; therefore, you are not feeling the benefits of your body and mind working in top shape.

All it would take is a few simple adjustments to have massive positive mental and physical results. How about we give it a try?

Here's the plan; it's simple. Try it, and feel the benefits. (Consult your personal physician before trying any new exercises or plans.)

Hydration

When your internal system is running better, you feel better.

THE PLAN

For women, this means 8 to 9 cups/day; for men, 11 cups/day.

THE BENEFITS

- Helps maintain blood pressure
- Increases brain power and energy
- Relieves fatigue
- Helps with weight loss
- Boosts immune system (best way to prevent colds)
- Prevents headaches (dehydration is the most common cause of headaches)
- Lubricates your joints (which help with minor back pain)
- Flushes out waste and toxins through urination
- Improves your mood
- Increases work or athletic performance

Lack of water increases your body's inflammatory response. Lack of water also increases pain sensitivity. Minor back discomfort can be because you are dehydrated. If you're wondering why you're not recovering from exercise, dehydration could be it.

Meditate

Meditation is almost so easy that we just don't do it. It's about prioritizing. Our minds can be the biggest obstacle in our lives; they get us off track and give us more negative talk than anyone. One tool to help overcome negative talk is meditation. Meditation helps clear the clutter in our mind and gives us clarity on things. When we have clarity, we are not distracted by the negative inner voice.

Make the time! "If you don't have 10 minutes, you don't have a life."—Tony Robbins

THE PLAN

Find the time! Even if it's 5 minutes, or even 2 minutes, make it happen. Here's how: find a quiet space, sit or lay down, and close your eyes. Focus on your breath and how your body moves. Observe how you feel before and after. You can even download a meditation app if that helps.

THE BENEFITS

- Reduces stress, anxiety, and depression
- Decreases blood pressure
- Increases attention span
- Improves sleep

Meditation is a workout for your emotional intelligence. It can help you relate better with yourself and others. It can clear your mind so that you can create, and it can help you "understand" yourself so that you can master your emotions.

Sleep

Too much or too little sleep can make for a tough day ahead. Keeping a regular sleep pattern by going to sleep and getting up at the same time daily will make you less likely to wake up groggy.

THE PLAN

Sleep experts recommend we get somewhere between 7 and 9 hours of sleep per day! Keep a consistent schedule. Try to get up and go to sleep around the same time each day whether it's a weekday or weekend. When you return to work, you won't feel so tired. If you're sleeping more on the weekend, then you're not sleeping enough during the week.

THE BENEFITS

- Lower stress

- Boosts your mood
- Improves memory, attention, and creativity
- Positively affects your physical and emotional health
- Lessens daytime fatigue and more stamina
- Helps you live longer
- Helps decrease anxiety
- Enhances your emotional stability

You build muscles, mind, and memory when you sleep.

Naps

Naps are so underrated. Some of the most influential and creative people rely on naps to refuel their energy and creativity.

THE PLAN

Take a 20-minute power nap. Set an alarm for 20 minutes. If it takes you 10 minutes to fall asleep, that's okay, but the total rest time should be 20 minutes.

THE BENEFITS

- Improves alertness and motor learning skills
- Reduces fatigue
- Increases alertness
- Improves mood
- Improves performance
- Quickens reaction time
- Increases memory
- Improves learning and working memory
- Prevents burnout
- Reverses information overload
- Improves sense of creativity
- Improves health
- Boosts productivity
- Helps to lose weight

Naps help build mind/body awareness.

Breathing

Breathing is a powerful tool to help us reset ourselves emotionally and physically. Generally, we take short, shallow breaths with our chest, which increases stress, tension, and aggressiveness, all of which can be relieved by taking deep breaths from our diaphragm.

THE PLAN

I use this technique during stressful times, but I also do it right before going to bed. Every day, spend time on your breathing. Take anywhere from 10 to 20 deep breaths by fully inflating your lungs, front and back, top to bottom. Figuratively speaking, take a breath so deep that it feels like you're breathing into your hips. Make practicing breathing a daily ritual.

THE BENEFITS

- Reduces anxiety
- Brings a sense of calming
- Improves your energy level
- Slows your heart rate
- Reduces muscle tension

Taking deep breaths is a great tool to resetting yourself emotionally and physically.

Visualization

I would guess that fewer than 1% of the population take the time to visualize at bedtime. Visualize who you want to be and what you want to do. Visualization can help build confidence and drive.

THE PLAN

When we lay down to go to bed, we usually think about the stress of the day or things we've said. Instead, focus on your dreams, goals, actions, and plans. Fall asleep with your mind marinating on your dreams rather than your stresses. Imagine how doing this for 8 hours a night will greatly affect your well-being, happiness, and motivation.

THE BENEFITS
- Improves performance
- Builds confidence
- Reduces stress
- Increases focus and chances of attaining goals
- Helps you relax

Brush and Floss

Take care of your teeth. According to a study in the *Journal of Aging Research,* taking care of your teeth with daily brushing and flossing can help you live longer.

Positive Attitude

Everything is more enjoyable with a positive attitude. Be positive. It will help eliminate doubt and build your confidence. It will help you cope with stress and anxiety. You have a much better chance of enjoying life more if you have a positive attitude. In life, you want to do everything you can to live a happy and fulfilled life, and it starts with a positive attitude.

Feed Your Mind

We work out our bodies, feed ourselves good food, and hydrate ourselves, but what do we feed our minds? Music, rerun shows, crime dramas? What if we took the time to feed our minds with positive influences, motivational and educational information, action plans, visualization, manifestation, intention, meditation, stillness? Pay attention to your thoughts and the information that you are feeding your mind.

You are probably doing some of these things but not to the point where they are offering positive results. Why not give it a try? Refocus, prioritize what you do with your time, and include these game changers? Try this plan and feel the benefits; it's that easy.

Note: The preceding advice is based purely on my experience and personal research. Before beginning any new physical program, consult with your doctor.

If some of the best athletes in the world have shown how doing mind work has made them the best at what they do, let's apply some of their mind/mental preparedness work so that it can benefit our everyday lives. As Michael Jordan says, "The mind work is what separates the great athletes from the good." Let's apply this every day and stand out from the rest.

Mind work can help you go from good to great in all areas of your life: fitness, work, relationships. Doing the inner work will change everything on the outside.

What a game changer.

One-a-Day Program

The following is a great personal growth program that I use daily.

I created this one-a-day program to help establish my daily rituals and to keep focused on what matters most in everyday life. One-a-days have been very effective for me over the years, and I feel confident they can help you too.

This exercise can be a tall order, so take action in as many categories as you can each day. The categories you choose should be the areas that are important to you, areas where you would like to see growth. The categories include work, health, relationships, hobbies, spiritual, bucket list, time for yourself, pets, friends, new friends, financial, and tasks you've been meaning to do.

Our lives are busy, but we must never lose sight of the things that are important. It doesn't take much to nurture the people and things we love. Sometimes, we tend to neglect the most important people and things in our lives because we are "too busy." This program will help bring the focus back to the most important areas of your life.

DO THIS:

Take a look at the preceding list; choose the areas that are most important to you.

Keep in mind you can add to this list. Write down one thing that you could do to foster improvement in each of them. Then, do them! Just imagine if you worked on one of these a day for the next year. That's 365 small things that can lead to massive growth within a year.

Establish a "One-A-Day" program. Take stock of the things that are important in your life and write them down. Start with these categories to help get you started, then add as you need to fit your life:

- Work
- Fitness
- Health
- Financial
- Spiritual
- Relationships:
  - Partner
  - Family
  - Old friends
  - New friends
- Bucket list
- Hobbies

- Travel
- Pets
- People to see
- Time for yourself
- Things you need to do

I remember going to bed one night and thinking about some goals I had for the Lazy Dog brand merchandise. I had a financial goal for the brand, and as I was going to bed, I realized, How do I expect this to happen when I haven't changed anything? I had to take some action if I wanted to experience growth with the brand. I had to come up with some action to make this happen. Every day for the next 365 days, I did something, anything, big or small, toward making this goal happen. Use the 365 program in any area of your life you want to change and grow.

Chapter 2

SUCCESS IS BEING HAPPY & FULFILLED

"Success isn't about how intellectual, funny, or personable you are, but about being kind all the while doing what you love."

I want to start off by talking about two things that you might think have nothing to do with success or business but that are actually the two things that can make you and your business go from good to remarkable: happiness and relationships. Happiness and fulfillment as they relate to success and relationships are at the core of every element of business. You will hear over and over the importance of your relationships and the people in your life. Great relationships and great people build great businesses.

Have you ever thought about what makes you happy or what makes you fulfilled? It's so simple, but I bet you've never written down all the things that make you happy (but you know we will now).

Everyone has a different idea of what happiness is. We think that if we are "successful," we will be happy. Reaching "success" goals will only make you temporarily happy. But focusing on being happy, doing the things you love and make you joyful, will make you successful. Be happy, and you will feel successful.

This is our formula for success at Lazy Dog: doing what we love, with people we love, and bringing more of the things we love into our lives and business that bring us joy, not as an ultimate end goal but as a way of life, every day. When you are happy, you are successful and everything is easier, including making money.

I find it interesting that when successful people are interviewed, they say they never felt successful until they gave back. Interesting. So, if the ultimate feeling of success comes from giving back, then maybe we should *start* our careers by giving back. Then, we start out by being successful, and anything that happens from then on is just icing on the cake.

The SCoop

Find something you are passionate about and then share with others.

Giving back can come in many forms: your time, money, advice. I love business, and so, sharing and giving advice to other people and companies not only helps them but energizes me by sharing something I love and helping others.

———

"The difference between success and not being successful is doing something. Take action."

———

DO THIS:
Let's Get Happy (aka Fulfilled)

This is a great and very effective action plan I learned from working with Jesse Itzler. We all define success and happiness differently. Let's see where your happiness meter is.

Action
On a scale of 1 to 10, how happy are you? Oh—you can't use the number 7. What's your number? _____

Write it down before you read any further.

Most likely, you thought of the number 10 and then thought about the things that are lacking and deducted them from 10. For example, maybe you think your life is great (10) but you are not in shape and want to lose weight and you have a work goal that you want to attain, thus making the number an 8. Whatever the things you list as your deductions are the things you need to focus on. These are the first things preventing you from reaching a 10, so give them priority every day.

List your deductions:

_____

_____

_____

_____

Give this list attention. These are the things that can help improve your happiness levels.

The Lazy Dog Path to Happiness/Fulfillment

It's more than simply knowing what to do; success comes from taking action. To make this more fun, write down your score next to each section (1-10, not using 7).

Take responsibility. Everything about you is *your* responsibility. It's always easier to look at others for blame. Even if it is someone else's "fault," look to yourself as to how you can change things; it's all on you.

Maintain a positive attitude. See the positive in everything. The more you focus on the positive, the more you will see, and the more opportunities will present themselves.

Choose your responses. If you don't like the outcome, change your response. Your response can change the result. It can completely change your life. It's that easy.

Do vs. have. Find happiness through experiences. Things only make us happy in short spurts. Things come and go, and they weigh us down. Experiences make you who you are, and no one can take away your experiences.

Get moving. Be productive, even if you are not where you want to be. If you are moving in the direction you want, you will be happier. For example, say you want to lose weight. Just taking the steps toward losing weight will make you feel happier. But it's in *starting* that you will feel happier. Progress breeds happiness.

Express feelings of gratitude. There are so many benefits to gratitude. Gratitude isn't as powerful when it goes unexpressed. Tell people how you feel about things and how you feel about them. Nothing new can come into your life if you're not grateful for what you already have. The easiest way to get rid of fear is to be grateful. The more grateful you are, the more wonderful things come into your life.

Say "I get to" instead of "I have to." This is a gratitude game changer. Notice the difference between "I have to go to work" and "I get to go to work." The latter brings us back to the ultimate gratitude that you have a work to go to. Pay attention to how much you say, "I have to" and then, switch it to, "I get to." Notice the difference?

Break societal/limiting beliefs. You are the one who holds you back. Don't let your thoughts or beliefs give you an excuse. Do it! Make things happen.

Change your perspective. Choose to look at things differently. It's so simple to do and becomes easier the more you do it. Believe everyone is coming from a good place with good intentions.

Trust in you. It's hard to be what you can't see, but trust that it's there. Visualize what you want. Don't worry about the how. The more you know and trust in what you want, the more opportunities will present themselves to you.

Be positive, but realistic. Phony happiness or being the "tough guy" suppressing sadness is not healthy. Find an outlet—a friend to talk to, a creative or physical activity—to help you transform the things that may weigh heavy on you.

Be your best self! Be the best *you*, not the best someone else. Don't imitate. You can't be a great someone else.

Transform the way you think. Be positive. Be kind. Your body has a physical reaction to your thoughts. Your body doesn't know what thoughts are real or not. Keeping positive thoughts will have a positive effect on your body.

Simplify. Declutter your life; too much stuff makes life more complicated. Getting rid of stuff gives you more time to bring experiences that make you happy into your life.

Forgive. Forgiveness is the strongest link to happiness. Ignoring the issue takes up just as much energy as addressing the issue, so tackle the issue, take the high road, forgive, and move on.

Perceive your reality. Positive people live in a positive world. More fun things happen by being positive.

Let go of the ego. The more self-absorbed you are, the more your life closes in on you, and it becomes harder and harder to find happiness.

Set intentions. Your intentions/goals will create your reality. Take the time to find out what it is you want in your life; then, start taking action.

Empower yourself and others. Keep yourself motivated and motivate others.

Surround yourself with the right people. Find people you admire, people who are giving, people who are kind. And surround yourself with them every day.

Chapter 3

CREATING YOUR PERSONAL CULTURE

"The better the culture match between the person and business, the happier and more successful the company and person."

Company culture is a well-known term in business, but personal culture is more important in your everyday life. **Your personal culture** is about being *who* you want to be and doing *what* you want to do. It encompasses your values and beliefs, how *you* think, act, and react. Spending time on your personal culture can bring clarity and happiness into your daily life. It can help bring clarity in sharing your company mission or help you find the right "fit" working within a company.

It's through your personal culture that you will feel an ease about life and creating your place in it. It's your values and beliefs and dreams and goals, knowing where you don't want to fit and where you do. Having a personal culture makes everything that much easier—your relationships, your job, your health, and your happiness.

I've read that people who are happiest at work tend to:
- align themselves with a company that fits their core values and beliefs.
- find a personal culture and create a job around it.
- be creative within their job and make a difference.

Culture is an imperative part of your success (as a business owner, employee, and in life). The better the culture match between the person and business, the happier and more successful the company and person.

When I decided to leave the corporate world and move to an island, I had no idea what I was going to do. Looking back, I can see I did have a clear personal culture. I wanted to live on an island, have a dog, and bring my dog to work. I wanted to create an atmosphere where I *wanted* to come to work, where I could hire my friends and they would want to come to work. I wanted to live by the ocean; share, empower, and bring joy into people's lives; make a difference; and have unlimited growth potential. Having a personal culture gave my life more focus on what I wanted and what I didn't want. Living by your personal culture, everyday opportunities arise that allow you to make it happen.

The SCoop

The more you love what you do, the more opportunities arise.

Having a strong personal culture, loving the outdoors, ocean, adventures, events, travel, business, and helping others has opened me up to more of all that: Being asked to be in The Explorers Club, to speak to corporations, to help put on events, to host events, to travel and participate in events, and test products. The truer you live to your culture, the more of it presents itself. It's in disconnect, being someone we're not or doing things we don't truly enjoy, that we get push-back and discord.

Defining Your Personal Culture

DO THIS:

Create and define a model for your personal culture in words that best resonate with you.

Answering the following questions will help you define your personal culture.

What's your vision of who you want to be?

What message(s) do you wish to send?

What are you passionate about?

Why do you do what you do?

What are your values? What do you consider important?

What are some of your personal beliefs?

What type of people do you want to align yourself?

What are the most important aspects of:
Family? Romantic relationships? Friends? Work? Health? Spirituality?

What environment do you want for yourself?

Where do you want to live?

What type of people do you want to work with?

What drives you?

What is unique about you?

What do you do? How do you do it? Are you firm, passive, easygoing, Type A?

What is your voice?

What brings you joy?

What makes you feel empowered?

What do you want to see more out of you?

Once you review your list, you will have a good pulse on your personal culture. Understanding your personal culture, knowing what makes you happy, and being aware of what you stand for all contribute to life fulfillment.

What Do You Want to Do with Your Day?

If life is made up of a series of days, instead of asking what you want your life to look like, start by asking what you want your days to look like. Are you doing what you want to be doing with your days? Don't think about what job you want; think about what life you want to live each day.

This is what I want you to always ask yourself when making a change. Sometimes, the change you think you want actually brings things into your daily life that you don't want. It's important to figure out what you want in your daily life and then, work a job into it.

> ## DO THIS:
> What do you actually want to do with your day?
>
> Start with the time you want to get up and then, break down the entire day to how you would like it to play out.
>
> _____
>
> _____
>
> _____
>
> _____
>
> _____
>
> _____

What If You Don't Know What You Want to Do?

I am often asked this question. Some people like their life but feel that something is missing. They know they are unhappy doing what they are doing. If you remember my story from the beginning of the book about quiting my job and moving to Key West, you will know that I didn't know exactly what I wanted to do. I only knew I wanted something different.

My friend asks her therapy clients what they were doing when they were 10. There seems to be a correlation between what you were doing when you were 10 and what brings you joy as an adult. At age 10, I was organizing events and games for everyone so that I could play—which is the same as creating a platform for people and myself to have great, memorable experiences.

What were you doing at age 10?

_____

The following actions and questions are some of the ones I used to help me find and do more of what makes me happy.

DO THIS:

You don't always have to know how to do something.

You simply have to make movements forward, and life will meet you half-way.

- Do everything. Sometimes, we find passion in things we didn't even know existed. This is based on the "say yes" action. Start saying "yes" to everything. Your world is bigger than what you know, so by jumping in and doing, you will find so much more than you ever thought existed.
- What moves you?
- What are you curious about?
- What would you do if money was not an issue?
- Find things you love and love to share and turn them into a business. What's your platform? Do you like to bake? Bake. How can you work this into your lifestyle and business?

- Meditate. Finding what you want from yourself comes from quieting the mind. Change, direction, and clarity will happen when you have stillness. If you don't know how to meditate, the easiest way is to find a peaceful, relaxing atmosphere, lay down, and focus on listening to your breath. Let your mind wander.

- Finding out what you don't like is just as important as finding out what you do like. Pay attention to both. In saying "yes," you will find things you don't like as well, so this will help narrow your focus.

- What drives your emotions is usually something that drives you. What drives you?

- Surround yourself with people you admire. Who are they?

Asking yourself these questions will start to build the platform for your new lifestyle.

When to Say "Yes" and When to Say "No"

If you know me, then you know my favorite word is "yes."

Say "yes," and then, figure out how to make it happen. It is always more fun to say "yes" than "no." You don't have to know how to do things; you simply have to say "yes." Not knowing how to do something is what holds a majority of us back, but jumping in, saying "yes," and figuring it out as you go by making adjustments as needed usually leads to memorable experiences in life.

Say "yes." When you're stuck, bored, or feel too comfortable, start saying "yes" to all that comes your way. This will open up your world; you will meet new people and have new experiences and opportunities. Saying "yes" is one of our core philosophies at Lazy Dog. It gives a feeling of, if we can, we will. "Yes" always leads to more fun.

The SCoop

The power of "No."

I recently found the power of saying "no." I was working with my Build Your Life Resume coach, Jesse Itzler, and he took our group though an exercise about our personal mission statements and goals. The exercise was about finding out what it is we want to accomplish in the next 200 days, focusing on how to do it, and then, when things come up during the day that don't align with our personal mission statement and goals, learning it's okay to say "no." This brings more energy into what it is we want to do. Saying "no" to things that don't align with the direction I am trying to take my business has brought massive growth in my projects and company.

One of my projects is to grow the Lazy Dog branded merchandise online. The brand has the biggest potential for growth within the company, and I really enjoy building a brand. But I keep allowing myself to be sidetracked by everything from opening a new retail location, to writing books, to speaking gigs and events. So, now, I'm doing everything, which is actually fun, but I'm not getting things completed. Saying yes, as fun as it is, only gets 80% of my projects complete, and then, I'm on to the next one. Saying "no" has helped me to focus and complete more projects and lets me still squeeze in a few "yes" responses. When it comes down to getting things done, bring in the "no" when things don't match your goals.

DO THIS:

Consider your personal culture, and formulate your personal mission statement.

You may ask, "Why do I need a personal mission statement?" A mission statement will help guide you and keep you focused on your life goals. Here is the action plan based on what Jesse taught me.

Take a look at the following personal mission statements to help you develop yours.

"To be a teacher. And to be known for inspiring my students to be more than they thought they could be." —Oprah Winfrey

"To have fun in [my] journey through life and learn from [my] mistakes."—Richard Branson

"My mission in life is not merely to survive, but to thrive; and to do so with some passion, some compassion, some humor, and some style."—Maya Angelou

Write your personal mission statement at this time and keep it short, clear, and concise at about three to four sentences:

Now that you have taken action and written your personal mission statement, you have a navigational point. When things come up throughout your day, if they don't fit your mission statement, consider how important they are and whether you will choose to do them. It is our personal mission statement that keeps us on course.

Chapter 4

UNDERSTANDING YOUR "BUSINESS" SELF

Entrepreneur vs. Business Person

"Not every business person is an entrepreneur."

Not every entrepreneur is a business person, and not every business person is an entrepreneur. A business owner is, well, the owner of a business! To me, being an entrepreneur isn't a role; it's more how you handle things and your personality traits. The number one skill of an entrepreneur is problem-solving, which, by the way, is one of the best skills a parent can teach a child. Teaching how to decipher information and consequences, how to make decisions and take action with confidence, and how to follow through. This also is the formula for making a great leader.

Entrepreneurs need to love and have the ability to problem-solve. By love, I mean you have to be the type of person who thrives on problem-solving because if you're not, you will end up a ball of stress. And by ability, I mean you have to be able to think differently, not just outside the box, but differently.

There are usually many ways to get to the end result. When dealing with problems, focus on the facts (take emotions out of the equation) and what you want the end result to be. I like to work backward in that I think about the end result, maybe what the customer wants or how I want the customer to feel, and *then,* I put things in place to make that happen. Focusing on the end result instead of the obstacles in front of you can help you think differently.

A few years ago, the Coast Guard told us they wanted us to cancel our paddle race around the island because of weather (very general). I asked them what their main concern was (specifically). They told me it was paddling around Sigsbee, which is on the Gulf side. For me, that actually happened to be less of a worry than the front Oceanside. Since that was the main issue, we revamped the course to avoid including Sigsbee, which changed things a lot but allowed the race to continue. The ultimate end goal was for people to race in a paddle race—and we achieved that. And fun was had.

Not everyone wants to be an entrepreneur; it's a tough job, but the rewards can be huge. There is something wonderful about putting in the hard work and knowing you are reaping the benefits, but there is also something wonderful about leaving work and not having to think about it until the next time you go back.

When you're creating, growing, and building a business, things will always pop up that you didn't expect. How you handle those issues can make or break your business. As I said, the best entrepreneurs are those who like problem-solving. But not only can they handle the problem-solving, they do it in style with a cool demeanor and creative thinking.

Entrepreneurs see opportunities in every problem. They find a new way to do things, or maybe they see a need to be fixed, or a product or service they can create to fill a gap. When others complain, entrepreneurs see an opportunity. Many times, this is how they create a business.

If you're an entrepreneur, it's important to remember that *you* decided you wanted to be an entrepreneur, not your staff or your friends and family, so don't make it their problem. In the early years when I shared problems with my staff and friends, they handled it worse than I did. I realized it's not for them. This is my job, and I will take care of it.

Can you train yourself to be an entrepreneur? Absolutely. With awareness, problem-solving techniques, and a positive attitude, you are well on your way. The following is a checklist that you can use to "train" yourself to be an entrepreneur.

DO THIS:

Do you have the core traits of an entrepreneur? Look over the following list and give yourself a score of 1 to 10 (1 being weak and 10 being strong) and not using 7 and see where you fall.

1. _____ You thrive on the ups and downs.
2. _____ You like to put out fires and fix things.
3. _____ You're even-tempered through all the ups and downs.
4. _____ You're comfortable with being uncomfortable.
5. _____ You're a strong executor; you can take an idea and make it happen.
6. _____ You're disciplined to work hard.
7. _____ You can see failure for what it is, a learning opportunity, and keep moving forward.
8. _____ You're willing to sacrifice making short-term money to invest in the long term.
9. _____ You're comfortable in the zone of the unknown.
10. _____ You like knowing your future is in your own hands.
11. _____ You don't blame; you fix.
12. _____ You don't complain; you fix.
13. _____ You're comfortable living in uncertainty.
14. _____ You see only speedbumps, not roadblocks.
15. _____ You're not a perfectionist.
16. _____ You don't hold onto the highs and lows in your life.
17. _____ You see a gap, and you see an opportunity, product, or service to fill it.

Review your scores. Anything lower than an 8 indicates an area you should focus on. A score of 6 or lower means you need some training. Prioritize and make the time if you want to be a better entrepreneur.

Drive the train or lay the tracks?

One of my most memorable interviews after college was at a shoe company in South Carolina. I interviewed with a very interesting guy to whom I could have listened for hours. He had recently come from Nike in Portland, Oregon, where he helped build a new division within Nike called ACG (All Condition Gear). To me, Nike was the pinnacle in sports, so I asked him why on earth he would leave Nike. He explained that there are two types of business people: those who want to drive the train and those who want to build the tracks. This has always stuck with me because I thought being an owner and enjoying my job meant that I liked driving the train, but as I look back on my business career, I realize the reason we are growing, moving, and expanding in many areas is because I want to build the tracks so that the company can continue. Once I realized this, I let go of the reins of the Lazy Dog operation so that I could build the tracks.

The SCoop

Working on your business, not just in it.

Bringing in people to take over many of my operational duties helped us grow over 120% the next few years. It then moved me into the next stage of my career and growth, which I wanted in order to help Lazy Dog and others build their business around the country. I want to share our business philosophy and help others build the tracks or drive the train. I want to feel that energy of something being built, help others, and, in turn, continue to build the Lazy Dog brand.

My manager, Kathy, drives the Lazy Dog train, taking care of the operational needs so that the company moves every day. My job in laying the tracks is to find tools, direction, and ideas to continually grow the company (and myself).

What do you want to do? Drive the train or build the tracks? Why?

DO THIS: WHO ARE YOUR 5?

Write their names next to each category and then call or text them and tell them "thank you."

Five People You Need

In a perfect scenario there are five people you need in your life to increase your level of success: Who are your 5?

Mentor – Someone on your same path but a few years ahead of you. _____

Coach – Someone to help with the day in/day out situations.
_____

Friend – Someone there for you through it all.
_____

Cheerleader – Your biggest fan to cheer you on in the tough times and celebrate with you during the successes.
_____

Devil's Advocate – Someone who takes the other side, asks the hard, challenging questions to help you better understand your purpose, your _why_.
_____

"Why" Can Change Everything

We all have ideas, visions, and dreams, but when you ask yourself why you want what you want, you may find those ideas, visions, and dreams change. If you have a strong "why," then you can have a strong business. Ask yourself "Why?" constantly. "Why" can change everything.

At Lazy Dog, I wanted to focus on building our merchandise line outside of our Lazy Dog Shack. I added a shoplazydog store on our website, linked it to Facebook, Pinterest, and Instagram, and then decided to sell through Amazon. I worked with an Amazon specialist who actually asked me why I wanted to sell on Amazon. You see, if my *why* was because I wanted to make money, then the products we were going to sell would be different. Plus, they wouldn't only have to be Lazy Dog products. But if my *why* was I wanted to build a brand through high-quality usable products that we use in our adventurous life that support the bond between dog and owner, then our products would be different. If my answer was to make money on Amazon, then I could simply be selling handbags (they are a top-seller on Amazon). But I want to build the Lazy Dog brand and keep it true to what it represents. Once this was decided, we were able to build a plan that fit my goals.

———

"Asking why will help you be more focused, inspired, and motivated."

———

A Job Is a Job; You Are Your Career

As in any job, learn as much as you can, grow, and develop relationships. Helping others at your job is a great way to do this. Appreciate your job, and if you find yourself complaining about your job—then find a new one (while you still have one). Your job is somewhere you go to learn, but when you are all filled up, move on. Find what you love to do because this is what you get to do every day.

People sacrifice so much of their lives, health, and relationships to a job. Take it for what it is. At this time in your life, if this is what you want to do, learn all you can learn, take your vacations, take your lunch break, but remember: it's a job. Jobs make you money; careers are what fuel and grow you.

Nothing Goes According to Plan

I'm not a big planner. I tend to jump in and figure it out as I go. I do this in part because, more often than not, what holds people back from "success" is not doing. So, I like to get that right out of the way by doing. Life isn't about doing things you know or you are good at—it's about doing things for their life experience. From these experiences, we grow, opportunities arise, and life gets fun.

The Formal Business Plan. Business plans are a waste of time and usually just a way for us to procrastinate because we are afraid. Business plans have no use unless you are trying to get funding from a bank or investors.

When working on a business or project, I usually write a 1-page business plan just to get my thoughts outside of my head. No fluff, just the important elements. I keep it simple so that it is easier to take action.

I have seen too many people get so caught up in a plan that they never start. Writing a plan is easy; acting on it is rare. Taking the steps to turn your plan into action is where you will need to dig deep to get started. Do one thing, no matter how big or small, every day to make it happen. Imagine the growth. Use the 365 growth plan from earlier in this book.

Stop procrastinating with a plan and jump in.

You *Can* Do It without a Partner!

When I was buying my second kayak company, the one that I had grown (for someone else) to the point that I almost couldn't afford to buy it, I needed a loan. I went to a local bank, went through all the formalities, and was approved for a loan. The loan officer then asked if she could give me some advice. She said she highly discouraged me from taking on a business partner. I told her it's okay because, "The person I want to go into business with and I are best friends. We went out the other night and drank a couple bottles of wine and told each other all our strengths and weaknesses."

The loan officer was right. A few years later, we are besties no more, following a lot of anger, tears, and jealously. We have since resolved our differences, but it was one of the toughest times in my life.

Did I need a partner? No, but I didn't have the confidence in myself back then that I do now. Advice I would give to my younger self is that you don't have to know how to do it—you just have to do it.

But I have no regrets. That partnership led me to where I am today. Everything happens for a reason, and nothing ever goes according to plan.

A One-Page Plan on Business

Here's the simple business low-down of the who, what, when, where, why, and how of business.

In life, we tend to make things more complicated than they are. It's like when we're helping someone else and are able to see the simple solution for *them*. But when the problem is our own, we tend to struggle to see a solution. Why is that? Because our emotions are tied into the situation. The following is an unemotional guide to business. Keep it simple, don't look for excuses, and make it happen. If I could write only one page of business advice, this would be it.

Who. A great business is built with great people. Find the right people, treat them as individuals, treat them with respect, and trust them by giving them the resources to do their job and act on behalf of your company. This will give them a sense of ownership and the freedom to do their job the best they can. They can't be a great you, but they can be a great them.

What. People are the key to any business. Great people can make a company with a good product better than a company with mediocre people and a great product. Have a solid product or service, hire great people, and give your customer more than they think they are "buying" to create a remarkable experience.

When. Well, as I always like to say, the time is now! Too much time is spent planning and re-planning. When has something ever gone according to plan? Jump in, execute, and adjust as you go.

Where. Everywhere! Market your business to all the sectors: fitness, arts and culture, travelers, business, schools, any segment you can find. And market across all social media channels. Be everywhere! Not just where you're comfortable or what you know, but *everywhere.*

Why. If you have a strong "why," then you can have a strong business. Ask yourself "Why?" constantly. You will find that when you do, your answer will be different than what you think it will be. "Why" can change your whole everything. "Why" can also help in communicating your company's voice to your employees and customers.

How. It doesn't matter if you don't know how to do something— just start. Make a move in the right direction, and you will figure it out. If we all knew the "how," business would be easy. It's the "how" that stops most people from fulfilling their dreams. Trust me; you don't have to know *how*, but you do need to take action.

DO THIS:

What's your why?

Write down something that you want to do, accomplish.

Now ask yourself why?

Ask yourself why again.

And again.

Keep asking until you get to the root of why you want to do something. What you may find is that there are many other ways to reach your why than you might have thought.

Ask yourself "why" as much as possible when making decisions.

Say you want to run every day. *Why* do you want to run every day? If the answer is to get fit, well, then, you can do so much more than just running to get fit. Asking why opens up the options to accomplishing the goal.

No one is going to hold you by the hand and do things for you. It's up to you. It's not easy, but it can be very rewarding. What are you waiting for?

Chapter 5

TACKLING THE DIFFICULT

"The best things in life are on the other side of fear."
– Will Smith

It all comes down to this: if you don't apply what you learn and know to your daily life, things will happen to you instead of you making things happen for you.

Some people are perpetual students, going from degree to degree. They learn, but they never put themselves in a position to apply their knowledge. People will learn what foods to eat to lose weight, they will read self-help books, or learn social media tools, but they'll never apply them. Learning is easy; applying what you learn isn't. This tool alone will put you apart from the rest. Always think, every day, "How can I apply this?"

If you don't apply it, it's like baking someone cookies and not giving them away. Or wanting to thank someone for something but not telling them. Or wanting to volunteer but not serving. In the end, even though the intention is there, nothing happens.

Think of it as an experiment; what's the worst that can happen if you follow through by applying what you learn or want to learn? You'll become happier? You'll have a life-changing experience? Give it a try and see what happens.

Identify and Eliminate Excuses

Excuses—I can't stand them! The worst excuse is, "I'm too busy." If you say that—then you need to take a good look at your life because your life is running you when you should be running your life. Things need to run on *your* time schedule. We all have the same amount of time, so stop using this excuse.

If you say, "It's just my nature" or —"This is just how I am," know that both of these phrases are cop-outs. Stop giving into this "nature" of yours and make yourself into someone you like. You can change this. Choose to drop your excuses.

DO THIS:

List your excuses.

What are some of your excuses?
I'll do it tomorrow?...
I'm tired?.....

_____

_____

_____

_____

What do you do to procrastinate?
Turn on the TV?...
Social media?

_____

_____

_____

_____

Find Your Fears and Act Courageously

Fear, like change, is a part of life. But fear can stop us from living our dreams. It often becomes a final decision for people, stopping them in their tracks, unable to move forward toward what they really want. Any and all fears that we don't tackle will run our lives. You can either adjust, move forward and grow, or you can just settle.

But it doesn't have to be that way.

Learn to play out your fear. What's the worst that can happen? *You will be okay.* When you're afraid, choose to learn all you can about that fear and conquer it. It's the unknown that adds to fear. The more we learn, the less fear holds onto us.

What's the best way to conquer fear? Take action. I heard Oprah say in an interview say, "Courage is feeling the fear and doing it anyway." I found this saying so powerful. See your fear as curiosity. Curiosity leads us to adventure. With curiosity and action, you can conquer pretty much anything.

It's like being in class and being afraid the teacher is going to call on you. Instead of sitting there not making eye contact and stressing, just raise your hand and tackle the fear. It's never as bad as we make it out in our heads.

Be aware of edgy emotions that are actually based on fear—such as anger, worry, criticism, and blame. These emotions are some of the demons that keep you from living out your true potential. You have a choice to come from a place of fear or of love. Choose love. It will change everything.

Everything you do and experience offers a lesson, even pain. Pain may slow you down, but don't let it stop you. Find a way to keep moving forward. And don't forget to invite in gratitude. When you are grateful, fear disappears and courage comes in, allowing you to control your own life.

DO THIS:

What are your fears?

List all of your fears, right now. Now, let's flip them around. Go down your list and see if you can find the curiosity in them. Ask yourself what the worst-case scenario could be for each one. Measure it against the best-case scenario. Do you feel less fearful?

Consider Failure

What does "failure" mean to you? I look at failure as, "Well, things didn't really go the way I wanted or thought they would." Other people might give up, but I don't want to be like other people. You shouldn't either. Instead, see what didn't work out the way you thought it would as an opportunity to learn.

To do this, you need to have the right attitude.

For me, it helps to take emotion out of "failure" and refocus. I take a step back so that I can see clearly. I'll ask myself, "What can I learn from this, and how else can I make this happen?"

Sometimes, I push right through, taking the hits but getting right back up, and sometimes, "failure" steers me in another direction, and it becomes something completely different—and sometimes, even better! But if I'm stuck in the emotion of the blows, I'll never see all the other opportunities.

If you have your head down and a too busy feeling sorry for yourself, you won't see all the opportunity. You can't move forward in life until you let go of your regrets and past issues. In general, I don't use the word "failure" because it's all just experiences that didn't go the way I expected but that I handled the right way. When you take the ego out of the outcome, stay positive, learn from the experience, and stay open to other avenues, you can grow immensely.

It's the ones who have failed many times who are the most successful and happiest in life, and they have probably experienced more in a lifetime than most.

Avoid Quitting

Quitting is not an option. Things may change. Maybe I'll take a step back to regroup, but quitting is not an option. I have encountered some tough times where I have wanted to quit, whether it's a paddle board race in crazy conditions, a business, a marathon, writing a book, or try-outs for a college soccer team. The main thing that stops me from quitting is that I know that once you quit something, the easier it is to quit and give up in the future. I have only "quit" one race and that was because I was delusional. I was stand-up paddling in a race 17 miles down the Na Pali coast in Kauai, in 4-6-foot swells. But then, the tailwind switched to a headwind, and the current was against me. I had run out of water, which is my kryptonite, and a boat came to ask me if I was okay. I said yes, I was just a little tired. I told the boat driver I was going to take a 10-minute nap and then continue, which obviously was not a good idea. He told me to get in the boat! It was a good call; I would have drifted out to sea. The question to ask yourself before you quit is how will you feel tomorrow?

The SCoop

It's Always Okay to Change Your Mind

I've made some mistakes over the years, and I guess some might say they are "failures" or regrets, but I look at them more as stepping stones to success because I learned from them, and they brought me to where I am today. One that really sticks out cost me $25,000. I'd decided to franchise Lazy Dog; I had been thinking about franchising on and off for seven years. Franchising involves so much paperwork and legalities that it's overwhelming, so I found a franchise attorney to draw up the documents. (You must use an attorney.) My main job was to write the operations manual. This was difficult because we don't work according to a manual. Lazy Dog is run on what I call "feel." Each person's interaction is different, and there are no rules or manuals regarding how to "handle customers." The manual was a must because other franchises would need to know how Lazy Dog operates. After about six months of my time and a $25,000 investment, we were ready. I launched our franchise program and was bombarded with applicants with questions such as, "How long until I don't have to work in the business?" or "How much can I pull in salary?" The people who applied were ones I had no interest in working with. On top of that, I had 11 layers of paperwork, back and forth, that was suffocating. My job had become one that I didn't enjoy. Yes, it would eventually bring in money, but it didn't fit with my personal or business culture, so I pulled the plug. It was a $25,000 lesson that I was able to put behind me and move forward with better focus on where the business was heading. It's never too late to change your mind.

Take Control of Finances

Finances are one of the stressors in life we tend to endure rather than do anything about. Take the time to focus on your financial goals; you can even meet with a financial advisor for some help.

Getting control of your personal and work finances can relieve a huge amount of stress. It can also help with goal setting and developing a clearer focus.

What's going on with your finances right now? Are you happy with the state of those affairs? If you are like many, chances are, probably not.

Our financial well-being can cause a lot of stress when things are out of balance, so it's important to take some time to think about your finances. Ask yourself some honest questions that will help you focus on what you want and the things you can do to improve your financial well-being. The following are only a few that helped me get clear and continue to help propel me into financial freedom and clarity.

DO THIS:

Take a few moments to consider the following questions, then write down your answers when applicable.

1. What do you want your finances to be like? How much do you want in your life financially? Be specific. And then, take the time to think about *why*. If you can't come up with a good "why," then you probably will change your answer.

2. What costs can you eliminate from your life to improve your financial picture? Can you make coffee at home instead of paying $5 each morning? Reduce your TV plan, adjust your cellphone usage, bike more/drive less, walk more/drive less? There are countless ways to get a handle on your finances.

3. What are ways you can earn more money? Save more money?

4. How can you automate your finances?

5. How much should you save and invest each month to get you to where you want to be?

6. How much are your monthly expenses?

7. When do you want to retire?

8. What does your financial picture look like? Visualize yourself having it all. I talked about visualization earlier in the book, and I have used visualization with my finances over the years. When you learn to visualize, you can begin to feel as if you already have what you desire. It's very effective and an important tool to practice using.

9. What other forms of income can you generate? Do you have a skill you can use on a freelance site like Upwork, Guru, or Fiverr?

All of these questions and more can help you relieve stress and create a clearer picture of your financial future and how to make it all happen.

Live a FIT Lifestyle

We want to be in peak and emotional physical shape, so you can put your best self going forward, every day, at work, in relationships, working out. Taking care of working out our minds and bodies is important. Doing so can lead to massive growth in all that you do.

DO THIS:

Begin to design your "FIT Lifestyle" by answering the following questions:

What weight would you like to be?

What needs to happen for you to feel good about your weight and fitness?

How fit would you like to be?

Was there a time in your life when you were fit and want to get back to? When was this? What were you doing then that you're not doing now?

What do you need to do to reach your goals?

What are the excuses you use that stop you from reaching your goals?

Where are your pitfalls in your food intake?

What do you need to do differently "in the kitchen" to help you eat for a fit lifestyle?

Life is supposed to be fun and successful, so keep everything light. The more you hold onto (good and bad), the heavier you become emotionally and physically. Keep it light so that you can soar.

Your life is your responsibility. You control your attitude, your reactions, responses, and actions. Awareness of these things can change your life.

Stop Coasting and Start Living

Being in a position where I speak to many people within a day, I have realized that many people are "coasting." They like their life, but they want to do something more. They want something for themselves. They want to sink their teeth into something. They just don't know what.

We often get stuck in a routine, and maybe we kind of like it, but routines eventually lead to ruts. Everything we do that "means something," that is impactful, takes sacrifice.

What I suggest is to "say yes." When someone asks you to do something, say "yes." This is the best way to get you out of a rut or to help you find the things that bring you joy.

Saying "yes" will take you places you haven't been before. Enjoy it, learn from it. Is there something you are afraid of? Tackle your fear. Enter uncertainty. This is where we shake things up to find out what makes us alive, what brings us joy. You dictate the pace. Are you ready to get out of your funk?

I can't stress enough, the more you jump into experiences (and whether you are good at them or not doesn't matter), the more you will live and learn about yourself. It's experiences that mold us into who we are. It's experiences that teach us, and no one can take that away from us.

You can be anything. When I was in college, I got mono and was told I couldn't be with the soccer team while I was sick. I was lost; the team was my "family" at school. I took a bus to visit my sister, Julie, who lived 30 minutes away. I sat with her and told her I wanted to quit school. She asked me what I wanted to do. I told her I wanted to be a lawyer. She got out a pen and paper and started asking me questions and writing down all the things I would need to do and what it would take to be a lawyer. I quickly realized it wasn't for me. Then, I said I wanted to be a professional triathlete.

She got out a new piece of paper and started making a list and saying it out loud. I again realized it wasn't for me, as I don't like to go fast on my bike, nor do I like to put my head in the water. What Julie taught me was that I could be anything, but the most important part was what it meant I was going to be doing with my day. Write it out, play it out, and ask yourself if this is really what you want.

You don't have to know what you want to do, only that you want something different. The more you do, the more experiences you have, the more you will realize what you want to do.

Thanks to the internet and great freelance sites like Upwork.com and Fiverr.com, you can try out different things and get paid for them while you figure things out.

Do the inner work. Ask questions.

DO THIS

If my sister Julie was sitting next to you and asked you, "What do you want to do?" what would you say? Write out below what you would need to do to make it happen.

———

"Everyone has potential; you just have to see it."

———

PART 2

Your Team

Chapter 6

BUILDING SUCCESSFUL RELATIONSHIPS

"Be the person who brings the energy to every relationship."

The single most important thing you can do to improve your business, personal life, and happiness is to focus on you first, then your relationships—business and personal.

It's the people, the relationships we have with all people—family, loved ones, customers, fellow employees, everyone—that can make you successful. If there is only one thing you are going to change—this is it, your relationship with yourself and with others.

What tends to happen for many is that we get so focused on doing our job that we neglect personal relationships. Nine out of 10 times, the person at the local grocery store, who does a great job at ringing up my groceries, doesn't look at me while saying, "Have a good day" when handing me the receipt. Our job is not merely the actual work. The job starts with a greeting and ends with a thank you, eye contact, and an acknowledgment that the other person exists. You never want a customer leaving feeling that they did you a favor, which happens at a few bars around. Give the people you come in contact the best of you, the best of your business, from beginning to end. There's a restaurant I visit that is very well known for its food and scenic views, but they put their "weakest" personable person at their host stand. This person sets the stage; they're the first person you experience when you come in and the last person you experience on the way out. Every time I eat there, the food is fantastic, the setting is like no other, but after I walk out without any acknowledgment as a person, I tell myself

I'm not going back. They don't make you feel good, welcome, or appreciated as a customer, and there are plenty of other places around town that do. Focusing on all the people in or out of work can change your life.

Relationships in business can take you from good to great. Relationships in your personal life can do the same.

I have always had solid relationships in all areas of my life, but at the same time, my core relationships were so comfortable that I did not always seek out new relationships. If I carry this over to my business, I will have a good customer base, but it won't grow. Your core relationships will keep you centered, but new relationships will help you grow. In expanding and taking the time for new people, or even people I see in my everyday life but didn't take the time with, I was able to experience the biggest growth I have encountered in my business and personal life.

The SCoop

Individual attention to any and all relationships will improve your happiness levels.

On a daily basis, I can see that when I take the time with people, there's an energy that surrounds us, an energy that improves our level of happiness. If you spend the next month doing some of the things I'm about to tell you, you will be happier, more fulfilled, and feel more successful.

What's more impactful than scheduling time for people is being present and accessible. I like to be around, accessible, and present with people in a more natural environment. For me, it would be heading into work when I don't necessarily need to be there to simply be present. To interact, listen, share, connect. If you are too busy rushing around because you're late or too busy working on your job to engage, you lose the ability to make connections.

DO THIS:
Relationships

The greatest gift we can give someone is attention and, in return, you can improve your business and life. Here's a great action plan that you can use in all your relationships.

Action
What relationships can you improve today? List the various relationships in your life.

_____

_____

_____

_____

_____

Circle the relationships you feel need improvement. Next to each relationship, write an action you could take to help improve it. Bring the energy. Make someone feel good.

Now, do it!

In some cases, this might be a big improvement, but do something every day to improve your relationships.

One of the most effective books I've read is called _The 5 Love Languages_. Basically, we all have a "love tank" that needs to be filled, and many times, this tank, is filled by people who try to fill it by "giving love" the way they like to receive love instead of how the other person wants to be "filled." For example, if you give someone a big expensive gift when all they wanted was a thoughtful, personal, handmade card expressing how much you love them, they won't be "filled." Give love the way the other person wants it.

Action
Make a list of the people you love and what means the most to them in receiving love. Then, list ways you can fill their love tank.

Action
List the 5 people you communicate with the most and write down their communication style.

The 5 Love Languages approach can be used for communication as well, be it at work or personal. How do individuals like to be communicated with (email, text, call, in person)? Use this approach in all you do; it will improve your relationships.

How to Improve Your Relationships

There're a few things I have found that really stick out when focusing on all relationships in work and in our personal lives.

BE AUTHENTIC

Being authentic means being real, being the best you and not imitating but creating. If you can be your true self and not an imitation of other people you like, you will have a more real experience in life. The right opportunities—the ones that truly fit—will come to you. Your interactions with people will have a deeper, lasting impression.

The better the relationships in your personal life, the better your personal life. Sounds simple, right? It is, but the outcome is huge.

TAKE RESPONSIBILITY

Take 100% of the responsibility for all your relationships, including the one with yourself. Your life is in your hands. No one is going to make you a success, make you happy, or create the life you want. It's all up to you. Once you realize that you're the one making all the decisions, it gives you a sense of power, of feeling that you can do what you need to create the life you want.

When you take responsibility for yourself, you don't have to rely on others to make things happen. Be open to support, but know how to do what you need to do. I've seen bright, energetic, self-motivated people who start to rely on other people so much (be it a business partner, employee, or personal relationship) and lose their "go-get-'em-ness" because the other person "takes care" of everything to the point that they no longer know what to do or how to do it. Keep your hands in the game and be responsible for knowing what you need to know.

"No one is going to take you by the hand and make things happen; it's up to you."

The Scoop

Taking responsibility in relationships.

I have learned a lot about relationships through Lazy Dog. Watching how customers treat one another, families, partners, kids and their parents—it's a great psychology experiment. One thing is for sure, the dynamic of the relationship is heightened as soon as you put two people in a kayak together. When there's another person there to take the blame, more often than not, we blame the other person. So, when I talk about taking 100% of the responsibility, you have lots of choices when you're involved in a situation with another person. You can stop, talk it out, and figure out a plan, or you can continue and get annoyed with each other.

If I trip over a toy that my dog left out, do I blame him? No, I tripped; I'm responsible. Taking 100% responsibility is not a common tool used by many, but it can completely change how you handle things and the ultimate outcome of how you feel.

I've increased my awareness around 100% responsibility and—*wow*—has it changed my life. It takes the negative energy out of situations and brings in ease. With this awareness, I change my reactions, behavior, and thoughts.

BE VULNERABLE

Vulnerability can greatly improve all your relationships. If you are willing to let down your guard and let people in, you'll see that it builds credibility and trust, opens the lines of communication, creates connection, breaks down barriers, and creates space for you to thrive. Ultimately, it shows strength and courage.

Vulnerability doesn't mean weakness, but the only way to find power in vulnerability is to be authentic, real, and human. To be vulnerable means to feel alive. Have the courage to be imperfect, to make mistakes. Know and embrace your weaknesses.

One of my favorite ways to be vulnerable is to open up and share stories about my experiences, good and bad. The following are a few ways in which you can begin to explore what it means to be vulnerable.

Embrace your quirkiness. Everyone has quirky behaviors—it's what makes us unique. Embrace everyone's uniqueness and your own. I remember when I was giving a friend a ride on my bike downtown to a restaurant, and she told me I was weird. I got really defensive and a little choked up. I thought I was pretty normal. She then told me weird is *good*; it means you're different from everyone else. Why would you want to be normal? A few weeks later, she gave me a picture in a frame of me with the following:

Adjective: normal; conforming to a standard; average, usual, typical or expected.
Adjective: weird; something that's unique, strange, awesome, crazy, or out of the ordinary.

From that day on, I embraced my quirkiness and that of others. Be who you are.

Acknowledge others who put themselves out in a place of vulnerability. When someone shares and opens up, give them props.

Share when you are uncertain (vulnerable). No one knows everything, so when you get in a place of uncertainty; it's alright to share. I thrive on doing things I've never done before, in business and in my personal life. I tell my staff, "I've never done X before, but we will figure it out."

Admit when you're wrong. Admit your weaknesses. It's alright to be wrong. Acknowledge, apologize, and move on.

Be kind. That's not the same as being right. Being kind overrules being right or having the last word.

———

"The more human you are, the better your relationships will be."

———

DO THIS:
Vulnerability

For the next week, try these relationship-improving techniques that focus on vulnerability. At the end of each day, reflect on the interactions you've had with others and write down what happened. How did it work out for you and the other person? Which techniques did you use?

ACTION
For the next week, try these actions out and watch how being vulnerable can improve connectiveness and relationships:

1. Share stories. It is the easiest way to let people in.

2. Acknowledge some of your personal quirkiness, some of the silly, fun things about you that make you unique.

3. It's better to be kind than right, so lead with kindness.

SHARE

Share with others. If everyone who turns up in your life is there to teach you something, then embrace every interaction and remember, that means you are showing up in *their* life to teach them something, too, so share. I believe that our purpose in the world is to experience, learn, give back, and make a difference by sharing with others. Doing so will not only be a gift to others, but it will be a gift to you as well.

Here are a few relationship-improving techniques you can lean into to help you cultivate stronger ties with the people in your life.

Focus on the people. This means the relationships you have with your coworkers, classmates, family, and friends. Where focus goes, energy flows.

Put your energy in people. People are your most valuable commodity in life.

Invest in people. Share, listen, and learn, and make time for people. A lot of people are too busy to spend time in their relationships because they're too busy being unsatisfied at their job and life.

Be influential. Make a difference in someone's day. It doesn't take much to show someone you care—a smile, a check-in, a call.

Be present. When you're talking to someone, be all in. Put the cellphone away and be in the moment with what's going on around you. If your phone rings, don't respond, and remember that the most important thing right then is the interaction you are currently having.

Treat every individual interaction for what it is—an individual interaction. Don't treat everyone the same. Ask questions, and let them talk to you. Everyone loves talking about him or herself. Ask more questions. Don't always relate everything to yourself; listen and allow space for others to talk.

Lead with love. It's hard not to be happy or grateful when you lead with love.

Take *full* responsibility for a relationship. A relationship is somewhere you go to give.

Break the pattern. Approach things differently. Get off autopilot and be aware of the people around you. Participate and share with people.

Relationships are where we go to give. Focus on what you can do for people, not what they can do for you. How many times have you said "hi" to someone, and they didn't respond? Then, you responded by muttering something under your breath. Did you say "hi" to that person expecting a response, or did you say it because you wanted to?

When I was younger, my dad and I used to run the streets before the sun came up, and any time we passed someone, my dad would say in his happy, chipper voice, "Good morning." Four out of five people we passed wouldn't respond. I asked my dad why he said hi to the same people every morning when he knew they wouldn't respond. He said it's because he wants to, and he's not going to let someone's response change his action. You control your response, your reaction; don't let it change based on someone's behavior. No expectations.

DO THIS:
Share

For the next week, try relationship-improving techniques that focus on sharing. At the end of each day, reflect on the interactions you've had with others and write down what happened. How'd it work out for you and the other person? Which techniques did you use?

There is that brief moment between an **action** and your **response** that can change your outcome. In that brief moment, bring awareness, take an extra second, and decide how you want to respond. This next action plan is so powerful to me because it shows you that you control the outcome. You've probably heard, "If you don't like the outcome, change your response." Well, here's a fun and life-changing action plan to make that happen. I use this in my workshops as a kindness practice, which it is, but I want you to become aware of how you can change the outcome.

BE KIND

DO THIS:
Practice kindness.

For the next exercise, imagine everyone with whom you come in contact, including yourself, is someone well-known to you, someone special or significant, like your best friend's mom.

To engage in the practice of kindness, try being gentle, actively listening, being patient, giving favor, being generous, and so on in all your approaches, reactions, and responses over the course of a week.

You may experience yourself engaging more with strangers and offering to help rather than looking the other way. You may also be much kinder in the way you respond to the people around you. For example, you may react less to a person who cuts in front of you in traffic. You may allow the guy behind you in the grocery line to go ahead of you because he has only one item. This takes awareness. What allowances would you make if you were more aware? What if it were your best friend's mom?

Notice these social interactions and notice your new responses after considering them as someone special. Notice the difference in how you feel and how your reactions begin to change with practice.

The easiest way to get happy is to put some energy into people. For the next week, be giving, positive, and engaging with people. You will see the immediate effect it has on your life. It will be a game changer that shifts how you proceed through life.

When the week is over, come back to this exercise and share what happened. Even if you are the only one to read it, in the long run, the act of reflecting and writing about it will help create the pathways to making it happen more often.

People Are the Product #gamechanger

A business is not the service or product that we sell; a business is in the people. By people, I mean you, the leader, staff, customers, and vendors. Great businesses are built with great people. When a customer calls and asks me what makes Lazy Dog better than one of the other companies in town offering the same service, I confidently say, "The people." Whether we are talking about leadership, customer service, marketing, or growth, the core of all we do is in the people. With that being said, relationships that you have and build become the backbone of your business. The more you focus on the people and relationships in your life, the happier and more successful you will be.

Chapter 7

CREATING A COMPANY CULTURE

"Company culture can make or break a
company and its staff."

Company culture consists of the philosophy, values, and behavior that constitute the unique style and policies of a company. It's a collection of beliefs and practices and the personality of your company—how your company thinks, acts, and interacts. It's important that you take the time to develop your company culture. That being said, culture revolves around the people *in the company* and how everyone treats one another.

At Lazy Dog, our company culture was built from my personal culture, one I had established before I had a business. Because Lazy Dog is a small company, my personal beliefs, values, and philosophies became that of Lazy Dog's.

The SCoop

Company culture can make or break YOU.

I remember reading a story about Tony Hsieh, the owner of Zappos. Tony built a software company with his friend; he loved what he did and loved going to work. As the company grew, he and his friend hired their friends, then their friend's friends until, eventually, other people were responsible for hiring. Tony came into work one day and realized he didn't know most of the people working there and didn't really like the vibe, so he sold the business. The $265 million he got from the sale probably made him feel better. He then started a company called Zappos, at which he promised himself he would never lose track of the company culture. His company even teaches other companies about developing company culture. Zappos went on to sell to Amazon for $1 *billion*. If you get a chance, read his book titled Delivering Happiness.

What does company culture do?
- Guides your company's behaviors, beliefs, values, and the morale of people within the company
- Creates an overall attitude of the company

Why is company culture important?
- Ensures brand consistency
- Creates a team atmosphere
- Improves staff morale for a happier and more efficient staff
- Facilitates hiring

———

"Great people make companies great!"

———

DO THIS:
Create your company culture.

1. Develop a mission/purpose from your company vision.
- What is your base message?
- What is something you're passionate about?
- Why do you do what you do?
- What's your vision?
- What do you want your company to become?
- How do you want your company to make people feel?

2. Define your core values. Core values are the backbone of your company, and they guide behavior.

Create a list of your values. What do you consider important?
- Behaviors
- Mindset
- Personal beliefs

Involve staff. Questions to ask yourself and staff when creating this list:
- How are we different from the competition? What sets us apart?
- What is unique about us?
- Why did we start the business in the first place?
- What do we do? How do we do it?
- Why does the staff choose to work here?
- What is the voice of our company?

Keep Company Culture Consistent

To have a healthy company culture, you and your employees will need to work daily to preserve it. When a new person joins the team, they need to be welcomed into the fold.

Develop tools to create a daily successful company culture.
1. Be consistent in your message. Does your message match your vision?
2. Tell stories; it is the best way to explain your company culture.
3. Write your core values down.
4. Have flexibility in structure.
5. Build and train your team.

How employees can contribute to company culture:
- Develop gratitude and positive mindset. Spoken gratitude is *powerful*.
- Lead by example.
- Support others' work.
- Offer praise and kind words.
- Focus on the positive, and you will find more of it.
- Understand the "what" and "why" of your boss and fellow employees.
- Support your boss and fellow employees.
- Develop strong relationships within your company (with everyone).
- Don't let the attitudes of your boss or fellow employees change you.
- Don't complain to co-workers, *ever*.
- Learn from negative behavior.
- Focus on the positive in people

Align yourself with a company of similar core values to your personal core values, and you will be much happier.

When you learn what drives your boss/company/employee, the entire company can communicate in a clear and effective way. Adaptation will occur swiftly.

Chapter 8

YOU'RE NOT A BOSS, YOU'RE A LEADER

"Leaders make decisions others don't want to make."

We all are, or have the potential to be, leaders. Whether you own a business, are the head of a family, on a team, part of an organization or group, 7 or 70 years old, all that matters is that you want to be a leader. How do you become one?

Start making decisions and then, follow up all your decisions with action. Leaders make decisions that others don't. They do things that others don't. They are less talk and more action.

The more tough decisions you make, the easier tough decisions will become. Making decisions doesn't mean you will always be right, but making a decision is better than not making one at all and sitting around doing nothing.

I think there is a formula for great leadership, and it all starts with you.

Leadership is about taking control of your life and exists in all elements of your life, not just at work. You can lead a company, team, organization, family, and, most importantly, yourself. Leaders know the importance of taking care of themselves *first*. By taking care of their needs, working out, getting proper sleep, meditating, and bringing a positive attitude and mindset, they then can put their best selves forward for everyone else without feeling depleted. When you don't take care of yourself and try to help and give to others, you become exhausted and drained. But taking care of you first allows you to be 100% every day. Anything less than that will negatively affect you, your staff, customers, relationships, fitness, and your business.

Not everyone is comfortable being a leader. Many are much more comfortable following the energy of others. But there is nothing more important for your own happiness, success, and fulfillment than leading your life the way you want. Becoming the leader of your own life takes some work. Find out what it is you want, create your own life, and make the decision to live it. Nothing will happen without action.

The SCoop

Anyone can be a leader.

My leadership abilities showed themselves when I was around 7. I was in the second grade, and my mom went to a parent/teacher conference. The teacher said I was incredibly shy and did not grasp some of the schoolwork but that I was a leader and my classmates followed me. Looking back, I can tell you it's because I didn't look to anyone else to create the things I wanted to do. If I wanted to play 4 Square, I organized a game. If I wanted to play Kick the Can, I organized a game. I didn't wait for someone to ask me to play. I created the platform, asked everyone to participate, and everyone had fun. I created the fun for my classmates and neighborhood friends, something that wouldn't have happened unless I decided to make it happen.

I took control of my own life, and I did it for the sake of fun. These were things I wanted to do. If I wanted to play, I made it happen. I didn't wait around for others to create the opportunities I wanted. Ever since that time, this has become my leadership motto: If it doesn't exist, create it. Don't settle for what's out there or wait for someone or something to present itself; make it happen. Take your life in your hands, give it direction, be proactive, and create it.

Now that you know you can be a leader, let me tell you how to be a *remarkable* leader.

The 2 Pillars of Leadership

My dad taught me at a young age that all great leaders and businesses are built on the pillars of trust and confidence, the trust and confidence you have in yourself and also in all those around you. Through trust and confidence, you build a safety net, allowing yourself and others to take the opportunity to excel knowing they will be supported. It's much easier to take chances when you know you have a safety net. Trust and confidence will encourage your staff to be self-starters. Productivity will increase, as will employee morale. Trust and confidence are built through, among other things, passion, work ethic, dedication, an understanding of people, a positive attitude, and consistency. In the following sections, I list a variety of ways to express these elements of great leadership. You will also see, over and over again, that self-care is a huge underlying component of what it takes to be a great leader.

As a leader, you need to be open to it all, even the things that you don't do well. Leave your ego out of leadership and allow yourself to be in a state of openness and learning with a willingness to change. If you want dedication, you have to be dedicated. If you want loyalty, you have to be loyal. If you want people to care, you have to be caring. If you want to build trust, you have to be trusting. If you want to build confidence, you have to be confident.

The SCoop

Letting go to grow.

For me to grow my business, I had to rely more and more on my staff to handle the day-to-day activities. At that point, they became the "face" of Lazy Dog, greeting the customers and taking them on adventures. If I trust them to do this very important part, then I absolutely must trust them with all other aspects of the business. Showing my trust and confidence in them to do what's needed only gives them more confidence, awareness, and pride in what they do. It brings a feeling of contributing to the growth of the company.

I have seen many businesses that "trust" their staff to be the "face" of their business but ultimately don't trust them with money or certain areas of the company. Distrust will bring down employee morale faster than anything.

DO THIS:

Rate your leadership.

The following is a list of things that are important to the Lazy Dog Way of leadership. Next to each section, write your score 1 to 10 (10 being exceptional, and remember, you can't use the number 7) on the line. After each section, write down one thing you can do to improve this skill. It might be something you can add, but it can also be something you can do less of.

Work Ethic

I'm going to say this over and over again: The way we do anything is the way we do everything. And if you are leading a company, household, team, or are in any other leadership role, you are setting the standards with your work ethic. Here are a few Lazy Dog ways to make sure your work ethic is on point.

Go above and beyond. As much as expectations can kill you and decrease your happiness level, many people have them. They come into a situation where they expect a certain outcome. If you can

give them more than they expect, you end up with a great exchange that sets you apart from the rest and propels you on the success track. Whatever you are doing in life, do a little more—whether it is in your personal or professional life.
What's your rating?_____

Always follow through and follow up. The task isn't complete when you finish it; it's complete when you follow up. This doesn't relate to tasks only but also to social situations.
What's your rating?_____

Stand by your word. People come from different backgrounds, upbringings, financial brackets, fitness levels, and educational experiences, but the one thing we all have is our word. So, when you hear that popular expression, "Be impeccable with your word," do it. Your word can define you. If you say you'll be there at 10 a.m. and are constantly late, no matter the excuse, you lose trust and value.
What's your rating?_____

Don't procrastinate. Do things now! Successful people don't wait until Monday. When you're moved to do something, do something in that moment, anything, big or small. Make any effort to move in the direction you want to go.
What's your rating?_____

Do the work you're asking others to do. One of the easiest and quickest ways to gain people's respect is to do the work you're asking them to do. Jump in when needed and help your staff. Be right there alongside them doing the work.
What's your rating?_____

If it doesn't work, try another angle. Be creative in your approach. There's always a way.
What's your rating?_____

If something isn't working, try coming at it from another angle. I've done this in my response to other people, to business situations, to how I study for a program. Don't give up because you ran into a problem. Successful people don't ever give up; they simply make a slight adjustment and try another angle. And sometimes, in doing this, a completely new door opens.

Just when you think you're done and want to quit, try another angle. REFOCUS. Most people give up too early. There are no roadblocks, only speed bumps. Obstacles are a part of life; tackle them.

Keep the word "no" to a minimum. "No" kills creativity and decreases morale. Whether I'm in a meeting or going about my day, I keep the word "no" to a minimum. Instead, think of everything as possible (because it is) and then, work toward making it happen. The word "no" stifles people's creativity and will also stop the people in your life—whether it is your friends, family, or your staff—from contributing because they don't want to hear it.
What's your rating?_____

Go back over your ratings, and if you wrote anything other than a 10, then these are the things you need to focus on to be a remarkable leader.

I apply this philosophy to my personal life as well as my work. Whether it's creating fun or leading a business, I lead and create for myself and others with a sense of passion and purpose. By doing what I love, I create opportunities and include others.

Create what's needed. Change the way you look at things. See the gap and fill it. Make it a win-win for all involved.

Understanding People

Understanding people, your staff, customers, vendors—anyone—can lead to massive growth as a leader and as a business. Here are some ways to help guide you to understanding people.

Care. Great leaders care about others. Caring for others starts by making and taking the time. I personally am always busy because I like to do things, but I *always* make time for people. This is key. What's your rating?_____

Recognize. See the individual within the team. You can't blanket-lead. I think this is the biggest downfall in leadership. It's about seeing people as individuals. Relate to everyone as individuals. Connect with them individually. Ask about their life and what they are doing, then follow up. What's your rating?_____

Communicate. Communicate clearly and effectively. Ask questions! Figure there will be some misunderstanding, so lean on the side of over-communicating, and while you're at it, explain why you are doing what you're doing. When there is understanding, everyone can facilitate in the process. I'm a visual learner, but not everyone is. Understanding my own "weaknesses" in learning and being dyslexic, I try to communicate in story. Explaining in stories really helps give the communication the "why." What's your rating?_____

Focus on people's strengths. Great leaders will focus on strengths, not shortcomings and weaknesses. Put people in a position where they can thrive, and the company will thrive. What's your rating?_____

Lead from love. Go through your day imagining that *everyone* with whom you come in contact is someone you love. If someone cuts you off in traffic and you yell at them, would you do that if it was your mother, or your friend's mother? No, you would react differently because you are coming from a position of love. Anger, worry, blame, fear—they don't work for us. Lead from love in all you do. We tend to waste too much of our time on petty aggravations, but when we lead with love, these aggravations don't get any time. What's your rating?_____

Connect. Get personal, take the time to get to know someone, ask questions, stop what you are doing and listen, make eye contact, and engage. Everyone's time is valuable, so show up on time and make the most of this time spent with people. If you're leading in business, don't forget to connect with your staff. Be accessible; encourage people to find you, call you, talk to you, and encourage them to bring ideas that will benefit the business.
What's your rating?_____

Deliver hope. Hope is a magical thing. Bringing hope to people can save them from misery. Hope is something every leader should strive to provide. Hope gives options, and options relieve stress.
What's your rating?_____

Empower and support. Empower and support those with whom you come into contact. Create opportunities for them to be involved and contribute. If they feel like part of the process/idea, they will feel more connected, grow, and learn. People will be more apt to be their best selves with this energy at play.
What's your rating?_____

Attitude. Be positive and find the best in people and situations first instead of finding blame. You can't change someone's attitude, but you can show them the value they have.
What's your rating?_____

Grace. Handle the highs and lows with grace and move on. Your attitude and emotions set the stage for your staff, so be graceful. Breathe in the highs, feel it, and move on. Breathe in the lows, feel it, and move on.
What's your rating?_____

Courage and the power of vulnerability. Vulnerability is an asset to leadership, building credibility and trust while opening lines of communication. It doesn't mean weakness. In fact, it shows strength and courage, breeding a multitude of assets that only the people brave enough to show vulnerability possess. Be *that* person.

Have the courage to be imperfect, to make mistakes, and embrace your weaknesses. Note when others are making themselves vulnerable, open up and share your stories, admit when you're wrong, and make apologies when necessary. The more human you are, the better your relationships, and the better your relationships, the happier you are, and the happier you are, the more successful you are.
What's your rating?_____

Get rid of your ego. Ego can be a business and relationship killer. Get yours in check. Without ego, you can learn and grow. Even if you think you know everything, listen to others. You might learn something, and others will feel good about sharing.
What's your rating?_____

Blame. Don't waste time trying to figure out who to blame when things go wrong, and instead, fix the situation and then, fix it so it won't happen again. One of my favorite stories on blame is from Ed Catmull's book, *Creativity, Inc.* Ed is the president of Pixar and Disney Animation. The animation team had been working on the movie *Toy Story 2* when someone hit a wrong button and 90% of the production was deleted. Instead of blaming and finding the person who did it, Ed gathered everyone together to figure out a solution. In that meeting, someone mentioned that one of the employees who was on maternity leave would come in each week and download the working production files onto her computer to work on them from home. They went to her house, got her computer, and only lost a week of work. If they had wasted their time on determining whose fault it was, they wouldn't have found a solution.
What's your rating?_____

———

"You can't treat your customers great until your treat your staff great."

———

Being Consistent

If you do anything, especially if you do it well, be consistent. Consistency in everything you do makes a great leader. Be consistent in your actions, reactions, and in your mood. Keep emotions neutral. Be consistent in showing up and doing things you say you're going to do. Consistency also breeds creativity because your staff will always know what they are getting from you, allowing an open and available energy for them to bring in new ideas and contribute.

If you want to be fit, then consistently work out. If you want to be healthy, then consistently eat healthy. If you want to build a successful business, then consistently do things to build and grow your business. It's easy to get sidetracked, but keep focused on the things that are important and do something toward making them happen every day.

What's your rating?_____

Awareness

Awareness could be a whole book on its own. This is one of the most important elements of anything that we do. Having awareness of yourself, of others, and of your surroundings can completely change how you go through life.

My father used to tell me one of the keys to his leadership style was that you can't blanket-lead; you need to treat *everyone* as an individual. How did he do this? By taking the time for the people he managed. If someone said they were going to a movie after work, the next day, my dad would ask how the movie was. Get involved in your staff's lives in a way that you know what they are doing and then follow up. This shows them that you are aware of their life after work and that they are more important than just the job. They are a person, and people are what make great companies.

We never know what is going on in someone's life; maybe th.
are some heavy things going on at home, which is why someon
acting out. Give allowances to people, don't react to their emotio
with emotion, and let them be without reacting to them.

It's a small yet busy space that we at Lazy Dog all work in, but
the staff have great awareness for one another. One of my favorite
examples is when we all show up to work. Even if it's busy and
people are waiting, we stop to give one another a hug because we
have appreciation and awareness for one another. Now, this may
seem strange to many, but we have been working together for so
long that we are family. We don't take this for granted for a second;
we are aware every day how lucky we are to work together.

A practice to obtain more awareness is to detach yourself from
emotions. Be aware of your emotions, but don't hold on to them.
What's your rating?_____

Taking Care of Yourself

Yes, we are back to taking care of ourselves. Remember, the more
you take care of yourself, the more you will be able to continuously
give, and in giving, you will receive, and the energy will be endless.

The other reason I say to take care of yourself is because this is
something you can control. If you are mentally and physically
tuned, you will never have to say "no" to adventures and
experiences. Personally, I don't ever want to tell someone I can't
do something because I don't think I physically can. This is in our
control. So, control it.

The following are just a couple of ways to start taking care of
yourself, but trust me, there are plenty more. Some of them can
be great fun, while others require a bit of focus and effort. Saying
"no" to a glazed donut and going for a run might be easy for some
and not for others, so it varies from person to person on what that
effort may be. But if you commit to yourself, you're well on your

way to being the sort of leader you'll need and want to be to mold your life into the shape you want it to be.
What's your rating?_____

Grow. If you don't grow your life, neither will your business. The key to growing is more than opening yourself up to learning; it's in taking what you learn about yourself and applying it to your daily life. Learning or thinking something won't make it happen. So, keep moving forward. Stay open. The best leaders take the time to grow, spending an hour or more on personal development every day.
What's your rating?_____

What do I mean by personal development? Anything that's going to enhance you mentally, physically, or emotionally. Attend a seminar, work out, listen to a podcast, meditate. You might be thinking that you don't have the time, but if you make the investment in yourself, you will prosper more than if you don't. If you are short on time, then listen to a podcast in your car, fall asleep to a meditation app, have a meeting while taking a walk, walk the dog without your cellphone, just be with yourself, or write in a gratitude journal. You will be healthier for it, and it will give you the energy to do what leaders need to do most, which is support their team.

Ask for what you want. I'm incredibly shy, and I don't do this enough. I come from the mindset that I don't want to put someone out. I have to work on this every day. I have unknowingly aligned myself with close friends who do ask for what they want and, guess what? They usually get what they ask for. Always ask; otherwise, the answer will always be "no."
What's your rating?_____

In general, you want to keep fit physically, mentally, emotionally, and spiritually. Fill yourself first. You can't truly give something you don't have in the first place. So, take care of yourself—you are the only one who is responsible for yourself. Don't look to others for this. It'll only lead to unhappiness if you do. I truly believe that if I take care of myself and fill my needs, then will I have unlimited energy for others. If I don't take care of myself, I seem to run out of steam. Get yourself in peak mental and physical shape so that you can best handle things as they come up.

DO THIS:
Get yourself in peak mental and physical shape.

Action 1
What can you do to take care of yourself? What will you do on a daily basis to take care of your needs?

Action 2
How can you get yourself in peak mental and physical shape?

DO THIS:
What's your leadership style?

Now that we've gone through the many elements of leadership, let's define your leadership style. Think about the great leaders that you know in your life and think about their leadership style.

Action 1

Who are your leadership role models in your everyday life (preferably people you know)? If needed, you can do this with role models you don't know (for example, Richard Branson and Sara Blakely). Think of who they are, pick four to five, then write down their names in the blanks below.

1.

2.

3.

4.

5.

Action 2

What do you like about the way they lead? What characteristics, personality traits, ways they handle themselves, ways they communicate, ways they think, act, and react stand out to you? Next, for each person, write down three to five things that you appreciate about them. Write down the answers to each of these questions.

Person 1: _____
                              (name)

1.

2.

3.

4.

5.

Person 2:_____
(name)

1. _____

2. _____

3. _____

4. _____

5. _____

Person 3:_____
(name)

1. _____

2. _____

3. _____

4. _____

5. _____

Person 4:_____
(name)

1. _____

2. _____

3. _____

4. _____

5. _____

Action 3
Now, look back at your list of what you appreciate about each one. Most likely, there are similar things on each list. Combine all four (or five) people and make a list of the things (without repeating traits) on the list. List them here:

There you have it, a list of the characteristics of the leadership style you aspire to become. You can use this list to help you fine-tune your qualities to be more of what you want to see in yourself. Keep this list around, remember what is important to you, and *become* your list.

Remember, it doesn't matter what your role is in life; everyone can be a leader. Lead your own life first by taking care of you. Take the time to figure out *who* you want to be, not *what*. A helpful tool in helping you find the "who" you want to be is to take the preceding Leadership Role Model action plan and do it again with people in your life whom you admire, your personal role models. This will give you an idea of who you want to be.

What Leaders Do

A leader's word is ironclad. I mentioned this earlier, but I want to hammer this home. We are all born with different upbringings and into different situations, but the one thing we all have, that we all start with equal is our word. What value you give to your word will increase or decrease your value. We can increase our value by being true to our word. If you say you will be there at 7 p.m., be there at 7 p.m. If you say you're going to do something, do it. There is nothing worse than not doing what you say you are going to do. What's your rating?_____

The SCoop

I am the top D.O.G. - Director of Growth.

One of the best managers I ever worked for was a guy named Greg. He was the VP at the footwear company where I worked. He arrived to work 2 hours before everyone else, did his work, and when everyone else arrived, he cleaned his desk and sat in his office outside the 40 desks in the main room. He had an open door and encouraged people to come in. He was there for whatever we needed: advice, ideas, support, or just to listen. At the end of the day when everyone left, he would go back to his job of growing the business. The company would never have made it to where it is without him. His method of management, realizing that people are the most important part of a business, that helping them, supporting them in any way to do the best job they can, was the best thing he could do for the company.

I have used his style as leader of the Dogs, as the Director of Growth. I work on the business—building, growing, and expansion—on my time. During the day when I'm at the shack, I am there for the staff. Whatever they need (support, advice, help, a listening ear, all in, whatever is needed)—that is my job, helping others.

Leaders think in solutions. Their focus isn't on problems; it's on solutions. Why waste any time complaining instead of focusing on a problem? Leaders skip that part and move straight into solutions. What can we do to fix this? What's the outcome we want, and how are we going to make it happen?
What's your rating?_____

Leaders fill the gap. When something is missing, leaders find a way to fill the gap, which could be creating a product or service. If it doesn't exist, create it.

What's your rating?_____

Leaders don't blame. Much like the preceding examples, leaders don't waste their time on blame but move right into "How are we going to fix this?" After we have moved past the fix, we can then look back at what happened that created the problem and what we can do to make sure it doesn't happen again.

What's your rating?_____

The SCoop

Find opportunity for growth in every interaction.

A customer wrote me a letter that said he had been paddling with us for years, and the last time he flipped out of his kayak with his phone and keys (electronic car key) in his pocket, both of which no longer worked. He put the blame on our staff saying that no one told him *not* to bring his phone and keys out in the kayak. I crumpled up the letter and threw it away. "Screw this guy. Come on, buddy. Really? You think it's a good idea to bring a cellphone in your shorts while you kayak?" But after awhile, I realized we are the experts at what we do, and some people don't know about what to bring and even what to wear when paddling. So, I decided to incorporate it into our check-in policy. And the response has been overwhelming in that there are *many* people who don't know that bringing a cellphone and electronic key out in the salt water is a bad idea. In addition, we started renting and selling dry bags and boxes to make it easier for people to bring their phones out paddling. This, in turn, created a huge new revenue stream. Thank you, Anonymous.

Leaders don't use excuses. There is no room in a leader's life for excuses. Take ownership, find a way to avoid letting it happen again, and move forward. No one wants to hear excuses, so don't waste your time. Allowing for excuses opens up others and yourself to more excuses.
What's your rating?_____

Leaders make decisions and then, take action. Leaders make decisions that others aren't willing to make. Does that mean these are always the right decisions? No. But they make decisions, take action, and adjust as they go. A "wrong" decision is better than not making a decision at all. The more you make tough decisions, the easier it will become to make decisions. A decision means nothing if it's not followed by action. Decisions become easier when you are more aligned with your values and beliefs in your projects and business.
What's your rating?_____

Leaders conquer their fear. Leaders conquer their fear by tackling their fear. No one wants to be afraid of doing or trying something, and the easiest way to eliminate any fear is to tackle it head on, thereby taking all the power and energy out of the fear.
What's your rating?_____

Leaders don't react; they listen. Leaders know the importance of not reacting with emotions. Instead, they listen, ask questions, and then, make decisions.
What's your rating?_____

Leaders are proactive rather than reactive. Making this adjustment can bring great growth to your leadership abilities. Social media has made all of us more reactive. We react to what we see, we get caught up in what's going on, and many times, this is happening right before we go to bed or as the first thing when we wake up. Shift to being more proactive, making things happen, and setting the path. We all have "that" friend who is always too busy running around; they are simply reacting to everything and

everyone. Set boundaries, schedules, and sometimes, you might even need to say "no" (My favorite word is "yes").
What's your rating?_____

The SCoop

If it doesn't exist, create it!

The philosophy of, "If it doesn't exist, create it" has singlehandedly changed my life, made me happier, and, in the process, made me more successful. It is an essential quality of mine, of Lazy Dog, and of everything we do. It's a mindset that can boost your creativity and carry over to all aspects of your life. Basically, everything is possible. If you want to do something but the tools to make it happen don't exist, create them. When you are plagued with the word "no" or "you can't do that," or even if you see things that you don't necessarily like the way they are done, make it happen by creating what you need.

Leaders don't let their emotions control them.
Criticism is not easy for anyone to take, but take it. Don't react. Don't get defensive. Be open and listen. Bite your tongue and take what is told to you and sit with it. When the emotions of anger, hurt, or whatever it may be settle, you will see the light. And the light may be that you can see where the person is coming from, and maybe you could make some adjustments or realize that the person is being totally ridiculous. But it's better to react without emotion. No one hears a word you're saying when you fly off the handle, and remember, you can't take back things you said out of emotion. Let cooler heads prevail.
What's your rating?_____

Leading by Being a Good Ambassador

To grow your business, you need to think much bigger than just your business. I want to be a good ambassador of the kayaking sport/industry and for Key West. It would be hard to grow a business that has a limited appeal, but if you can grow the industry you are in, then you can grow and expand with the industry. I feel this way about Key West as well. If I am good ambassador for Key West and make sure people have a great time during their stay, then it can help increase tourism, bringing in more people and more potential customers to Lazy Dog.

I look at growing my business in four parts:
1) I personally need to continue to grow as the leader of the company because then, the company will grow.
2) I want to grow Lazy Dog as a company.
3) I want to grow the industry that I am in, in this case kayaking and paddle boarding.
4) I want to grow tourism in Key West.

The SCoop

Create your customer.

When I first bought paddle boards for our rental fleet, no one asked to rent them for about two years. Then, slowly, people would rent, but the paddle board growth was still slow. When I asked people, even my friends, if they wanted to try them, they would say it looked too hard. People were not going to try something they thought they couldn't do and pay for it on top of that. So, on the last Sunday of the month, I would trailer our entire 16-board fleet down to the beach and give free stand-up paddle board instruction and let people play on the boards. Each Sunday, the gathering grew and grew. Some people would just come and watch, but once they saw someone do it, they'd say, "If they can do it, I can do it." The next month, that person would be out there.

Although the instruction was free, it was a great marketing tool. But even better than that, we were turning people on to the sport. We were creating our new customer base. Shortly after that summer, we doubled our fleet to 32 boards, and I've never had a problem renting them again. We grew the industry within our community. The paddle board customer base didn't exist, so we created it!

Business growth is much bigger than focusing on your individual business alone. Look at the big picture, be a good ambassador for your industry, and grow the industry, grow your city, and grow your business into the new growth you have created.

Your attitude as a leader will dictate the culture of your company. If you are inspired by passion, have a great work ethic, take the time to understand people, and have a positive attitude, then you are on your way to being a great leader. You have a choice every day regarding your attitude, so make the right choice.

DO THIS:
What's your Leadership Rating?

We need to determine where we are to get to where we want to go. Not everyone knows where they want to go in life, but we usually have a strong feeling about where we are currently. Let's take a look at your leadership and where you want to go.

On a scale of 1 to 10, how do you rate yourself as a leader? You can't use the number 7.

Write your number here before you read any further:_____

Most likely you thought of the number 10 and then thought about the things that are lacking and deducted from there. For example, maybe you think you're a great leader (a 10) but you could communicate better or spend more time being present with your staff, thus reducing your score to an 8. Whatever reduces your score are the areas you need to focus on. What are they?

Prioritize the things that are keeping you from a 10 every day.

Onward and Upward

The only way to continue being a good leader is to be sure that you are constantly growing yourself. If you don't grow, the people "following" you won't grow, and then, they will move on. As a leader of a company, without any growth from the leader, people will quit. And the company will become stagnant. Keep moving onward and upward, and everyone and everything will follow.

Chapter 9

ASSEMBLING A STRONG TEAM

"Great companies have great people; remarkable companies have great teams."

Building and creating a strong team within your organization (be it a business, association, church, team, and so on) is a key element of great companies. In my experience, it's where you go from good to remarkable.

Everyone wants to be part of a team, to feel part of something bigger than themselves, to contribute, to be included. There is a sense of belonging when you are part of a group, be it a team, a company, a church, or association. Belonging brings people a sense of worth, it brings comfort and security, and it also brings the ability to take more risks. When people feel part of a team, they are more apt to contribute to the team. There's a feeling that the company is also theirs, a sense of ownership, and when someone treats something like their own, you know they are taking care of the business and will go above and beyond. There are many people who have never been part of a team, but if you've been part of a team, it's a feeling that we take for granted.

The SCoop

Great teams don't just happen–they're created.

I was a part of a sports team for most of my first 30 years. Being part of a team is second nature for me. But it wasn't until I was in my 40s that I realized there are some people who have never been part of a team or group. As I was growing my business and developing paddle race groups and teams, I saw the transformation of some people from individuals to team players. They became more empowered, confident, and happy to be part of a group. There is a sense in a team of belonging, of looking out for each other, a togetherness rather than being alone. Once I realized what was happening, I focused on deepening and expanding the teams and groups. The comradery, confidence, and progressiveness of these people were amazing. I truly believe this is when my company went from good to great in its culture and financially.

I recently saw an interview with a professional football player, a rookie, who was 24 years old. He was asked what team he would play for if he couldn't play for his current team. He chose the Rams, and his sole reasoning was because of the coach, its leader. He said the coach cared so much about each player, treated them with respect, and had such a passion for the game. He gets in the trenches with the players, cares, and is expressive and respectful. He wanted to play for someone like that. Everyone wants to be treated with respect and for who they are. The best leaders do this.

If you want your staff to care, then you have to care. You have to get in the trenches with them and show them that you're going to do just what they're going to do, and you're going to lead the way (although, sometimes, you're going to have to let them do it themselves). You need to have trust and confidence in them that they can do that, but sometimes, you have to be in there with them to remind them how much you care so that they will too.

Team Building Fundamentals

There are simple ways to build incredible teams, and ultimately, they revolve around awareness and the individual within the team. The following is a list of some of the tools I've used in developing the team approach in all areas of my life.

Believe. First and foremost, a leader MUST believe in their people more than they believe in themselves. This is the single biggest growth tool a leader can use.

Listen. The best way to include your staff is to let their voice be heard. This also increases morale. Listen without always responding. Take it all in. Give space and allow people to talk.

Encourage people to contribute. You want your staff to feel like they are a factor in the company's success. Bring them in, explain what you are trying to accomplish, and explain why. I have seen many companies in which employees are told what to do without understanding the *why*. Explaining the why brings your staff into the rationale behind the business and opens their creativity and willingness to contribute. Encourage them to communicate, share, and act on ideas.

Use staff input when hiring. Your staff is there for the day in/day out of your business, so you want them to like the person you are hiring. Let them be part of the process. If your staff is involved in hiring, they are also most likely to invest in that staff member. When hiring new staff, I usually have them go out on a tour so that they can see what we do. The two hours spent on the water with a Lazy Dog staff member is usually a good indicator for a potential hire.

Share with your team when you change things or have new ideas. Explain why you are changing things. In general, change makes people nervous, so explain why.

Have equality. From a customer's point of view, there are no job titles. Everyone can do everything. When a customer comes up for a gift certificate, to place a special order, or even a refund, any Lazy Dog staff member can handle any task. It's a team, not a hierarchy. The best way to achieve this is by empowering through resources.

Empower through resources. Since the beginning, I have used this approach to leadership. Training and trusting my staff to be able to handle any situation that arises gives them the confidence and empowers them to do their best. In return, a customer can be treated to the best care at all times. Teach your staff how to do everything. That way, if a situation comes up, each employee has the resources and know-how to get things done. Remember the two pillars of building successful businesses? Trust and confidence. Empowering through resources will do wonders for building your pillars.

Hold yourself to high standards and be consistent. If you do, others will too.

Open the door by being accessible and consistent in your personality. This opens the door for people to be creative and bring in ideas on how the business can do better. This is easy for me because we literally don't have any doors, just a picnic table and open shack.

Communicate within the team. I use a 3-part communication style because everyone learns and hears differently. Write it out, speak it, and then tell it in a story. The story helps give understanding.

Know your strengths and weakness, as well as those of your staff, and put people in a place where they can thrive. And fill in your personal weak gaps with people who excel where you need help. There is nothing wrong with having a weakness. Know it and fill the gap with others who are strong.

Promoting, hiring, and moving people into positions that don't match their strengths is a common problem that I see at many businesses. People will take a promotion because they are moving up and it usually comes with extra money, but if you end up in a job that you are no good at or don't like, then it's a waste of everyone's time.

Make considerations for your staff's lifestyles. You want your crew to be happy. It's not a lifestyle for only you; you want to make it one for them too. I tell my staff they can have time off as long as they give enough notice. We prepare our schedules a month at a time, so once it is set in stone. It is then up to the employee to find their own coverage. There's a lot of talk about Millenials how they want to feel needed, want to work when they want… Honestly, this is how we have been running our company from the beginning. It's not about Millennials; it's about allowing people to have their life. The happier people are in life, the happier they are at work.

Embrace all personalities. Let people be themselves within the job. It becomes more authentic, and customers will feel this. Plus, people function better when they can be themselves. No one can be a great Sue Cooper (except me); I want them to be a great version of themselves at work.

Work on the business, not just in it. Your staff's job should be more than merely working in the business, so give them projects to work on the business in order to be part of its growth and success.

Get involved. The more involved you get yourself and your crew in your goals, the easier it is to make decisions that lead the group as a whole toward the goal.

Create a creative, freethinking environment. A place where it is okay to be wrong, where it's okay to ask for help. This creates a team of contributors. At Lazy Dog, we have a wooden picnic table where the "magic happens." It's where we take a break, wait for customers, eat lunch, socialize, and sometimes talk business. It's a comfort zone in a relaxed atmosphere. People can come and go, freethinking, having ideas, thinking big, and never using the word "no." It's where most of our ideas come from. People are comfortable at the picnic table; it's a creative zone.

Grow. If you don't grow your business, you won't grow, and your employees won't grow or stay with you. Don't be complacent.

Put people in the right place. Once you find the right people it's important to put them in a position to succeed. Some people work well with open, flexible, creative schedules. Others might need a long to-do list to check off as the day goes.

Let people grow. Now, it's extra motivation to grow the business so that the staff can keep growing financially *with* Lazy Dog. As our company grows, new jobs within the company open up. As we grow, I remind the staff that anyone can move into any role if they want. They can create their own position as long as it is something that we need.

Never take away what you give. There is nothing that will make an employee feel more defeated than when you take away something you gave them, such as reducing their pay. I have seen this in other companies, where the company goes through a downward turn and reduces the employees, pay even though they are doing the same work. It's deflating and can be a company morale killer.

Be there for your team and cultivate that mentality among team members. One of my employees, who is also one of my closest friends, is Bethany. Sometimes, when things get crazy at work and I ask her to help in an area where she wasn't scheduled, her answer is always, "I'm here for you, whatever you need." Her attitude is so great because she is a team player. But as fun as the job is, it is a job, and she respects that and does the work. I've only had a few employees who didn't seem to respect the fact that this was a job; they didn't last long. I see many other places where people don't seem to have any respect for their job, and it comes off as if they are doing a favor for the owner or, worse, for the customers. It's like seeing a customer going into a bar and ordering a drink and the bartender gives off a feeling like he is doing the customer a favor by getting them a drink. I love sitting there and watching; it's so entertaining because it is absolutely ridiculous. When a customer prepares to leave, the bartender gets irritated if he doesn't get a 20% tip. Tips are for good service, not per transaction.

You and your staff are a team, so act like one. Work together and don't let your team down. Teamwork doesn't seem like work.

"You can't go wrong when you hire good people."

Hiring to Grow Your Company

Hiring good people can be easier than you think. I have found over the years that hiring has nothing to do with experience and everything to do with the type of person *you* are. People who are kind, motivated, and personable will always have a place with me over someone who has no people skills and relies on their "qualifications" only.

Hire good people, people who like people, people who can relate to people, people with awareness of other people and themselves and train them in the job. There is nothing more valuable than authentic, personable relationships between staff and customers. This is how we do it at Lazy Dog, but this can and should be done in any relationship-based business.

This is what you, the leader, need to do to make hiring and keeping great team members easier.

Company culture needs to be organically you. You need a solid, clear company voice/message. This will attract people of similar values and beliefs. The clearer your company culture, the easier it will be for you to find and hire people who have a similar culture, leading to hires who are happier, more productive, and less likely to quit.

Be a great leader. Remember what I said earlier? The best leaders build a company on trust and confidence. These two things will encourage your staff to be self-starters and then, productivity will increase (you'll need fewer employees) and employee morale will increase.

Respect your staff. Offer your staff additional hours first before seeking new employees. Give them first choice.

Referrals. Ask your staff for recommendations. If an employee recommends someone, that employee will tend to feel invested in the new hire and help them.

Keep your staff in the loop. Keep staff involved with prospective employees. They will be working with this new hire, so get them onboard. How can your staff help?

Strunking. Yes, I made this word up. Strunking is my personal secret to hiring good people. I go shopping, and I pay attention to the staff, such as how they interact with other staff, with customers, and themselves. I am very aware of staff when I'm shopping or at a restaurant. If someone is good at their job, I let them know I'm hiring. This is one of the easiest ways to find good employees. You get to see them in action before you hire them.

The SCoop

One of the hardest parts of the job can be the most profitable.

One of the hardest parts of a growing business is when you take yourself out of your role and replace yourself with other people. You feel that no one can do the job the way *you* do. To grow, you must trust other people to do your job. In my second year, I was forced into this because I broke my leg and didn't have anyone else to handle tours. A girl I knew saw me on crutches the day I broke my leg and asked if I was hiring. It was meant to be. Michelle became my first employee. I quickly realized that being out of the day-to-day work meant I was able to grow the business. I then hired Michelle's friend Julie, who became my first full-time employee.

When paddle boarding became all the rage, paddle businesses were booming everywhere. There were two pieces of advice I gave often:

1) Do you want this to be a hobby or a business? If you want it to be a business, then jump in full-time. Make the commitment.
2) Hire someone, even if it's for 1 day a week, so that you can work on your business instead of in your business. This one is so hard for people. Take the short-term hit for long-term growth.

Back in my corporate days, I could always tell whether someone was going to "make it" or not. I was so good at this that the woman in charge of interviewing new hires would have me sit in on the interview. I could tell whether the candidate was excuse-driven or would do what was necessary. Excuses don't make things right. If you were late to work because of traffic, the bottom line is, you were late to work. No excuses. What are you going to do so that this doesn't happen again? Do what is necessary.

The Question to Ask Every Potential Hire

What If *You* Ran the Company?
The one question that you ask your employees or potential employees can tell you a lot about them is this:

"If you were running the company, what would you do?"

The ones who have big, unrealistic plans are the ones who want a quick gain, "I would pay myself more money." or "I would hire more people." These are the people who don't want to work harder and want more money and time off. These are not your long-term employees; they are actually the ones you want to keep an eye on, and not in a good way. The ones who say, "I would offer more events, add a program for youth, update the employee manual," and so on are the ones who are looking to improve the company. These are the ones who are actually *adding* more work for themselves and the company. These are the people you want to keep around. They care about the company, not just themselves.

Givers, Takers, and Matchers. Givers give more than they receive and do things because they need to be done, not because of something they are getting in return. Takers take more than is given, asking "What's in it for me?" And Matchers will give back only what they receive.

I personally want a to hire a Giver but one that takes my lead. It's my nature to give out of respect, and I hope my givers respond in the same way. Givers will get equal if not more back from me. I will do anything for my staff. I don't expect my staff to give before I give first. Leaders lead the way. If you give first, love first, accept first, then you open the doors for others to join you. If you wait until it's the other way around, it most likely won't happen.

I love my staff; they have my heart. I love who they are, and I love that they treat my business like it is their own. By providing the support, resources, trust, and confidence so that each employee can make the best decisions throughout the day, they work hard and treat people and one another with kindness. One of the best compliments we get at Lazy Dog is how great our people are.

How to Get a Job with Me

There is *only* one thing that we consider in hiring someone at Lazy Dog: do you like people? Are you nice? Are you a good person? It's a difficult task to teach someone how to treat people with respect and kindness and have it come across naturally. If being kind isn't your true nature, I'm not interested in hiring you. Maybe someone can fake being kind to a customer, but that will only lead to talking behind their back to the staff, and that's a whole other problem.

The SCoop

My tips for job hunters.

I remember in my early 20s when I was applying to companies. Of all the places I wanted to work, professional sports teams were tough places to apply (there's no turnover, and it's all about who you know). I remember telling myself that when I had a company, I'd hire everyone who applied. Not the smartest or most experienced, but the ones who showed self-motivation, who were not afraid to do things differently, and people who are nice. (You can't teach someone who isn't nice to be nice, and in a customer service-oriented business, "nice" is important.)

Well, obviously, hiring everyone who applies is not realistic. So, I've decided to fulfill that commitment I made to myself to "hire everyone" by giving you advice on how to get a job with me, most of which you can apply to whomever you are applying with. It's simple. Here are the three steps:

1) First, research the company you're applying to and its key personnel.
2) Second, find out where they are heading, what they're putting their energy into, and what they need.
3) Third, find a way for you to fulfill their needs.

Simply put, if you research that we're trying to expand our Lazy Dog-branded merchandise line through our online store, and you have skills that can assist in this expansion, then that would be the focus of your cover letter. Look at what a company is doing and explain to them through your experience and skill what you can do to help them. What if you don't have skills in online marketing? Then be creative! How else can you help us expand our brand?

Now take that advice and apply it to wherever you're job hunting. And if you're hiring? Snap up candidates that show they've done these three things.

Create your job. Then, if you're successful, you're solidifying your position within the company.

I have had some wonderful people (and some very close friends) ask me for a job. "When you're ready for me, Sue, I'll come work for you." Basically, they are asking me to build a job for them. That's not the type of person I'm looking for. I'm looking for someone who will create a position that we need to help me grow the company. "Sue, I know you're looking to expand your brand, so how about I research all the top Florida festivals and events where we could showcase our brand?" or, "We could set up a program for college students to work the events to cut down on travel costs." Find a way to create and justify your job.

The SCoop

The wrong fit will feel like it.

Many business books recommend hiring slow and firing fast. This is not me. With a small staff of 16 to 20, we are tight, like a family. I've only had one situation that pushed me to the limits, which was a guy who worked for me for four years and who was great with customers but not so much with the staff. I eventually found that if I assigned him to do tours solo, it seemed to work. However, on occasion, he would have to work with others. After he got off tour with one of our core staff members, who is the complete opposite of him in personality, he asked me to fire her. He gave me his reasons, was hotheaded, disrespectful, and would not back down. No good decisions come from heightened emotions, so I told him to take two weeks off and that we would revisit this conversation. I was close to saying something that I would regret. Taking a step back and not getting caught up in his emotions was a great tool for me that day. One I have used in all areas of my life since.

After two weeks, he and I went down to the dock and sat down. He spoke first, "Did you think about what I told you?" I got up and said, "You're fired." He went to work for all my competitors but never lasted more than a month with any of them.

The SCoop

Why firing fast is important.

There have been a few times that I have felt I'm walking on eggshells in my own business because of staff personalities that don't "work." I first try to figure out why they don't work; maybe it's as simple as someone is not a morning person, so I should give them afternoon tours or maybe it's other personality conflicts. I try to find the fix before moving on. Or I find what it is in me that makes me feel like I'm walking on eggshells. This kills company culture and needs your attention immediately. I fire too slowly, telling myself that they are great once they get going. But that's not enough. Even if it's just a few hours here or there, the moodiness affects everyone—me, the staff, and the customers. It kills culture.

Red Flags

If you see new hires doing these things, get them out of your business—fast.

Entitlement. You know that feeling when someone makes you feel they are doing a favor for you by working for you? Yeah, see ya!

Tardiness. This is a big one for me. Tardiness shows a lack of respect for me and the others who are working. Communication can lessen this blow by letting us know you will be late. However, in a small company, tardiness doesn't fly. It affects employees as well as customers. This is one of my biggest pet peeves in business and life. Being late shows a lack of respect, period.

Attitude. Not only do I expect you to come to work and do a great job, but you need to come with a great attitude all day. I don't ever notice a "good job done" with a bad attitude. Attitude is everything.

Moodiness. Moodiness can create a very uncomfortable environment at work. Moodiness isn't personal, it could simply be that someone isn't a morning person. But you see, this is a job. It puts other people on eggshells and isn't good for the culture. If you were in a Broadway play, you wouldn't let moodiness get in the way of your performance. Don't do it here either. Act it out!

Know-it-alls. If you aren't willing to listen, even if you think you know the answer, you're out.

Condescending. There is never a time to be condescending. See Ya!

Passive Aggressive. I've got no time for you.

I. There is no "I" in team; there's only "we."

Millenials Are On to Something (born 1981-1996)

Much has been made out of Millennials, much of which is negative. The "way" Millennials want to work is how Lazy Dog Adventures has been running since the beginning: treat everyone as individuals, be respectful, work together, be involved in the growth, make a difference.

Millennials get much of the media attention and rightfully so — they will be 35% of the workforce in 2020 and 75% of the workforce in 2025.

For starters, I want to share with you a list of characteristics that summarizes our Lazy Dog staff as a whole. Our team consists of baby boomers, Gen X, Y, and Z ages 16-58 years old.

- To make an **impact**, change the world, make a difference.
- To make **decisions**.
- Be **appreciated**, every day.
- Are motivated by the prospect of creativity, change, and social interaction rather than pay raises and climbing the ladder.
- To make instant connections with people.
- To progress, not because of climbing the ladder and money but because they will get bored.
- Freedom and space.
- They want to feel like their place in your business has meaning; if it does not, they will leave.
- They want access to bosses, to be mentored and coached, and for bosses to show an interest in them.
- They will sacrifice pay for a better work/life balance.
- Instant feedback (thanks for social media).
- To adjust their work schedule to fit their life rather than the other way around.

By the way, this list is also how media describes a Millennial. So, obviously, we don't make too much of "Millenials" as we all want to be appreciated, make a difference, have balance...

In Lazy Dog fashion, let's not look at the issues; lets focus on solutions. How do you manage a millennial or a Lazy Dog staff member (no matter what their age)?

- Explain how what they are doing is making a difference.
- Give them projects to work on with fellow staff.
- Let them know how their projects affect the company.
- Say thank you!
- Ask about their personal lives.
- Explain the vision of your business. They want to know that their work matters in the scheme of things, that they are a part of something larger.
- Allow them to use social media.
- Give freedom and space to make decisions.
- Treat each as an individual.

- Allow decision-making as a group.
- Create opportunities for volunteer and charity work.
- Give them very good direction and let them run.

Where the big adjustment in business needs to be made because of Millennials is from a sales and marketing perspective. Millennials create a great opportunity for us all. Why?

Because Millennials are a $2.4 trillion market.

Now, how are we going to market to them?

- Advertise in their space, which is social media space. Pay for Instagram ads or Google ads that appear on YouTube.
- Advertise by using visuals (pictures and video that's real, not staged) in places where people can like, comment, and Tweet). Millennials are much more likely to buy because of their peers' recommendations, so put your products up for all to comment on.
- Millennials are emotional; connect with them through story. How can you create a story that tugs at their heart?
- Millennials want to know that they're being heard. They value relationships, so take the time to embrace the relationship.

We want to make it as easy as possible for people to pay, and so, we have always accepted all forms of payment. With Millenials, we have to continue this, as cash is usually the last form of payment a Millennial will use, preferring debit cards, Venmo, and Apple Pay.

Chapter 10

LAZY DOG MANAGEMENT

"Manage people the way they want to be managed."

The best managers are the ones who understand people and their personalities. It's about people. Great leaders manage people the way people want to be managed. If you take the time to understand who you are working with, you can create an environment where they can excel. The more productive the personnel, the higher the company morale and the fewer the people who are needed to work and the less turnover you'll experience.

When the company began to grow beyond what I could do, I knew I needed to hire a manager. In the past, I was the one who hired everyone and was the go-to, but in hiring a manager to do this, it was imperative that my management philosophy on how to treat the staff be communicated. I hired my friend Kathy. Kathy and I are very different personalities; she's organized, task-oriented, and is a clear communicator. I needed this, and our company needed this. I am an idea girl with 20 balls in the air and who works more off of feeling rather than tasks. Because my style is different from Kathy's, we needed to find a way to best merge our styles. I personally believe that the best managers are the ones who understand people and their personalities, managers who take the ego out and embrace the staff to be authentic and to bring their personalities out. The staff's uniqueness is what will connect with customers. Whether it was Kathy leading or me, our management philosophy would be the same: manage people the way people want to be managed. How do we do that?

Language of communication. The best way to communicate with your staff is by doing so in three ways. Some people's strength is listening, for some it's reading, and some need it in context. So, what I do when trying to get information, points, or philosophy across is write it down for people to read, explain it in person, and then, most importantly, share an example in a story. I give the message context and make it three-dimensional. Stories help to share the reason, the feeling you are trying to accomplish.

The main job of a manager is to manage people. Your job is to take care of those working with you. It's not for you to get reports done; you can do that later. You want to create the best team possible, and great managers have great people working with them. Managers take care of their employees. That is their primary job. Working on your business is done on your own time, not on your staff's time. When the staff is around, your job is to support them. When you are on your own time, work on your business and grow it.

Treat employees individually and with care. People are the most important part of your business, so treat them with respect, allow for their personalities, and treat them all as individuals. Listen, ask questions, and care about what is going on in their lives. Follow up. Never blanket-lead. Treat everyone as the individual that they are.

Know when to work on and in your business. Don't work on your business when it's busy with customers. This is a time to be present and support your staff.

Stay connected. Always know better than anyone else what is going on within the company. Know if there are personnel issues, customer stories, posts on social media (flattering and unflattering), and how much money you grossed that day. If you're not around, then no matter how hard you are working, your staff will start to think you don't care. You have to keep connected.

Model the behavior you seek every day. You set the behavior levels for the company. Be, act, and speak the behavior you want to see out of your staff. It's important to be consistent in this behavior; otherwise, it won't stick.

Fixing small problems is priceless. As a manager, you probably have many balls in the air, lots to worry about, and some of the more minor issues that your daily employees deal with might not make a big difference to you, but it might to their everyday life. If an employee has an issue that needs addressing, even if you don't think it is that important, addressing it, fixing it, whatever it takes, shows that employee that you are about the business from top to bottom and that you care about them, and this is priceless. Take care of their needs so that they can take care of your business.

Management isn't about being a person's friend; it's about treating everyone as individuals, with respect and kindness, something we should be doing in all areas of our life. It's about making people feel good. It's about believing in people.

DO THIS:

Find your management style.

Who are the best managers you ever had in your work life? List 3 to 5 managers you like and what you like about them. Review the list when you're done, and you will most likely find the style of manager you aspire to be.

_____

_____

_____

_____

How to Find Your Number 2.

There are certain qualities that you want to find in a number 2, a second in command, your right hand. Having the right number 2 means finding someone you can trust, someone who treats the company like their own and who ultimately doesn't want your job but wants to be a number 2. They have all the control, but when push comes to shove, they don't have to make the big decisions.

Here are a few key things to look for when hiring a number 2.

Fill the roles you don't like. When I hired Kathy, my main objective was to find someone whom I could trust to take over the part of the business that I don't like, the books. This is one of the first roles to hire because it requires a lot of time, and it takes the leader out of their role by making them sit at a desk doing the numbers.

Close the gaps of number 1. No one is perfect, even if you are a number 1. Understand your weakness and hire a number 2 that can fill the gaps.

Different talents, same goal. The best number 2s will have different skills than the number 1. Different skills brings harmony and completeness to management, whereas same skills bring friction.

Do your magic. Number 2s let the number 1s roll and do what they do.

Trust. This is the ultimate qualification. Find someone you trust with the inner workings of your business and mind.

Understanding. Understanding the number 1s culture and message and help convey that message.

All great companies have solid number 2s. Find yours, and it will make business much more profitable and fun.

Be the Leg

Sometimes, I work at Lazy Dog from the home office or under a palm tree. When I'm at Lazy Dog, the staff knows I'm there to help them. I am "the leg" to provide whatever they need that's going to make them more productive and happier at their job. It could be picking up a customer in the van, gassing up the boat, calling a concierge, or picking up a staff member for work because her bike had a flat tire and it was raining. No matter how big or small, be there for your staff so that they can excel at what they do. Not only am I doing something that they appreciate, but it shows that I care. There is nothing that will build employee morale quicker than caring.

DO THIS:

What can you do for your staff that would greatly affect their daily job?

If you can't think of anything, then you're not there for your staff, and you need to be. Trust me, it will improve your overall business and morale.

DO THIS:

What is your staff's language of communication?

Write down your staff's names and describe how *they* like to be communicated with, not the way *you* want to communicate with them.

Now, take the same list and write down a way you can relate and communicate with them better. What can you do as their manager to communicate better?

_____

_____

_____

_____

_____

_____

_____

_____

_____

_____

How to Earn Respect

During one of the first seminars I gave, someone shared, "I have a busy paddle company, pay my employees well, buy them lunch, and they just don't listen or have any respect for me." You can't buy respect. Respect will come from your behavior, and the easiest way to build respect is to get hands-on and do as much, if not more, than anyone else. If I'm not willing to jump in where I'm needed in a moment's notice, then most likely, the staff won't either. If I'm not willing to stay late, then others won't either. It starts with you. Be all in and lead by example; there is no better way to build respect. Respect doesn't come with words. Respect comes by leading through example and doing more than anyone else.

Fundamental USA

Business can be easy, but it's human nature to make it more complicated. We overcomplicate our work, our relationships, and our lives. I'm a big baseball fan, and Big League players go to spring training at the beginning of each season to ramp up for the season. How do they do this? By getting back to basics, to the fundamentals of the game, so that they can maximize their skills.

Shout out to Keith Kneeland who brought the term "Fundamental USA" into light. Lazy Dog had a co-ed softball team, and during one game, the other team kept running, and we kept over-throwing the bases and throwing behind the runner instead of where they were running to. Keith brought the team together, told us to take a knee, and then said, "Fundamental USA people!" Back to the basics, the fundamentals, we went, and it changed the dynamic of the game. We were so caught up in the game itself, and the emotions of the other team doing whatever they wanted, that we lost sight of the basics, the things you *must* do to succeed.

As I walked across the parking lot into work the next day, I thought about the fundamentals of business and came up with the following. When you take out all of the layers of complication, it boils down to this, which is what was important on day one of the company, when it was just me, to 21 years later, with 21 employees. The basics of business, the fundamentals.

No matter what level you are in your business, it is sometimes easy to forget the basics. Here's your fundamental USA routine drill.

1) **Answer the phone.** Businesses spend a lot of money on advertising to get customers to call, so if a customer calls you, answer the phone. When I first started, I checked the phone all the time to see if it was working. I was so excited when the phone rang because it meant I had a customer. It's easy not to answer the phone when we get busy, but it's just as important when we are busy as it was when I first started. It is a customer calling. After payroll, advertising is the next biggest expense. We advertise to get people to call us, email us, and visit us, so when they do, ***answer***.

2) **Don't park where your customers park.** If there is no parking nearby, a customer might drive right on by. Don't

park in a spot that makes it harder for a customer to visit you.

3) **Don't be so busy working *in* your business that you neglect the customer.** This is the most common problem I see in my personal shopping experiences. Everyone's too busy working to help customers.

4) **Be on time.** There is no room for tardiness. All it shows is a lack of respect for other people's time.

5) **Keep your word.** Do what you say you are going to do; there is no more valuable currency than your word.

6) **There's a beginning, middle, and end to every customer conversation.** The more you can engage with a customer, the more likely that customer will return. Even more important than what you do is how you make your customers feel. The transaction isn't over after the customer pays. Keep engaged at every level.

7) **Hire good people who understand the value of people.** Hire people who can organically connect with others. You can always teach job skills to people, but you can't train good, authentic personal interactions.

8) **Take it when you can get it.** Every business has to start somewhere. When I started the company, even if only one customer called to go kayaking, I took them out. You have to start somewhere, and if that one customer has a good time, then they will, hopefully, tell someone else and maybe even return another time. With a new business, you have to take what you can get. But in any business, when you have a customer, make the sale. If you've closed your store and are about to get in your car to go home and a customer asks you if they can buy something, well then, *open the store*. We spend so much money on marketing and advertising, why would you ever turn away a customer?

9) **"I'll be right with you."** When growing a company, you don't always have the time or staff to take care of everything. Things get neglected. In our case with our retail store, I noticed that everyone was so busy, which is good. But when a customer would come into the store everyone was so busy that nobody acknowledged them. We spend money adverting to get customers and then, they walk in the door and we are too busy for them. It is like a customer service center not answering the phone. How are you going to sell anything if you don't pay attention to your customers? Acknowledgment is the key. Even if you are too busy, you should always acknowledge your customers. Just a simple, "I'll be right with you," whether it's on the phone or in person, will give you extra time. People like to feel like they are being taken care of. Make them feel good by noticing that they came in; directly or indirectly, it says, "Thank you for coming in [or calling]. I will be right with you."

Where do you rate on these elements of Fundamental USA?

The SCoop

Be available or pay someone else to be available.

When I started out, I had my cellphone with me 24 hours a day because it was the reservation line. I brought the phone with me everywhere, even on a run. I had a guest house call me to set up a kayak tour for some of their guests. The rep from the guest house said she would like to set us up as their featured trip because she said whenever she calls to make a reservation, I answer the phone. She doesn't want to call around to find someone to answer the phone to make a reservation for a guest. It takes up her time and the guests' time. It is so simple; answer the phone. These days, if you don't answer the phone, the customer will move on to someone who will.

The SCoop

Make it easy for people to buy from you.

One customer came in my store, put down a bunch of items at the cash register, and said, "Do you take Discover?" I said, "We take it all, whatever you want to give us." He said, "Well, that's refreshing; you would be surprised at how many places don't. I don't understand why a place of business wouldn't take all forms of payment." This has always struck me. Why would a business not take Discover? Because the credit card fee for the business is higher than Visa/MC? Are you willing not to take Discover and potentially lose a customer?

The SCoop

Find your place in the band.

Fairly recently, we were going through another growth spurt, which is always appreciated but which can bring some issues as well. I have an amazing crew, and as we've grown, I have always told my staff that I want the staff to grow too. As new opportunities arise, I want the staff to move into them if they so desire. Although I don't like job titles at Lazy Dog (I prefer each person to be able to do everything), I needed to have some clarity as to where everyone fit within the company.

My best friend Holly, who has worked in another field, has helped me run our events over the years. As time went by, she's helped more and more until she ended up working for me. She is my best friend as well as my confidante in everything personal and business. She helps me with everything as well as being my person to bounce ideas of. I just didn't know where she fit within the business; I already had an "operations manager" and a "daily manager."

A friend and fellow business owner explained the importance of "the band" exercise. She said to imagine your company is a band. Ask your staff, "If you were in a band, what would be your role?" And yes, this will be your next DO THIS action. I asked my operations manager, and she said she would be the drummer. She keeps the beat, keeps everyone in sync, but every now and then, she wants a drum solo. The clarity and understanding I had of my operations manager became so evident. She was just that. And I was missing an important part of her job by not giving her the drum solo. She is so good at what she does, she's behind the scenes, and I need to give her the spotlight every now and then to show my appreciation. I need to make sure that every now and then, she has her well-deserved drum solo.

When I asked my best friend, she said she's not in the band. She is an independent songwriter. She is very detail-oriented and wants to make sure she puts together the perfect song so that the band looks amazing. She won't do anything subpar, and she cares so much about the band. This answer helped me understand her role and understand her so much more. I did this "band" exercise with my entire staff, and it was a great tool for understanding where everyone saw their role, what they wanted out of their role, and matching it to where I saw them. We were able to spring forward from there.

DO THIS:

Ask your staff this question: "Imagine the company is a band. What is your role within the band, and why?"

Write down their answers and what you can do to make that "band member" fit their role.

(blank lined note area)

With most of my staff's answers, I realized two things:

1. Most people don't want to be in the spotlight, but they do need a solo every now and then. So, give them their moment to shine.

2. Realizing that most people don't like being in the limelight helped reinforce that I am the leader, and I chose to be in this role. Not everyone likes that role, and not everyone is an entrepreneur, so don't put them in positions and situations that don't work for them. Some people are solid employees, but few are entrepreneurially-minded people who what to run their own business. And since they didn't choose entrepreneurship and you did, don't force your problems and situations on them. An entrepreneur handles the problems; the employees work.

PART THREE

YOUR BUSINESS

Chapter 11

BUILDING YOUR CUSTOMER BASE

"Going beyond customer service."

My dad told me that IBM built its business model not on customer service but on customer *satisfaction*. This was ingrained into my life at an early age, it was even engraved on the pencils my dad brought home from the office that were all over our house. Customer satisfaction is a large part of Lazy Dog's success.

Customer satisfaction can excel when you have one thing: authenticity. Authenticity will lead to a deep customer connection and improved customer service that will lead to high customer satisfaction.

4 Keys to Customer Satisfaction

Listen. People like to talk about themselves and feel good talking about themselves. Leave them feeling good about you and your business by letting them talk and them feeling like you listened. Listen as people give you the information needed to help you connect.

Connect. Take what you learn by listening and connect with the customer. The focus is on them. If they have a problem, solve it. This is not about selling them your product; it's about making a connection.

Engage. Look at them as if they are the only ones in the room and you have the time to engage them because they are important.

Share. Share something of yourself to solidify the connection. Don't switch the focus to you but do share. Sharing is where we build relationships.

Since our level of customer service was high, I decided to focus on customer satisfaction. Customer satisfaction can be hard to achieve if you are too busy doing your job. I actually hired another person to work during our busiest hours. The reason was because I wanted to make sure our entire staff had the time to LISTEN, CONNECT, ENGAGE, and SHARE with our customers. I didn't want our staff to be too busy doing their jobs. They all know that part of their job is to listen, connect, engage, and share. If a staff member sits down and chats with a family after their trip, I know they're making a connection. And here's the thing: it doesn't work if you're not authentic. You need to have people who work for you that are organically your culture, authentic, and love what they do.

Having repeat customers is a sign that you are doing things right, that you are building your business; the money will soon flow in.

Where I see many companies fail in customer satisfaction is what happens after the initial greeting/check-in. There is usually a disconnect between after the greeting/check-in and before the service as well as after the service and before the check-out. This is where companies can easily improve their customer satisfaction rating by getting involved with the customers, conversing, connecting, applying the 4 keys of customer satisfaction.

The sale is made once you receive payment, but the customer becomes a loyal customer through following through. Don't lose the connection while they are in your place of business.

In relationship businesses, you have been given the beautiful gift of being put in a position to make a difference in someone's life. And it starts with LISTENING, CONNECTING, ENGAGING, AND SHARING.

DO THIS:

What places that you frequent are you a loyal customer of and why?

Make a list and include these reasons to complete your customer service plan by solidifying the loyal customer.

Love your customers first. Gary Vaynerchuk of VaynerMedia tells one story about loving your customers. You have to love them first. Think about parents and their newborn child. Parents loved their children before their children could love them back. By loving them, they, in turn, love you. Gary suggests using the same philosophy with your customer. Love them first, and they will love you back.

Living in a tourist town, there is competition for almost everything out there. So, when a customer calls and says they have three brochures in front of them offering kayak tours and asks, "What's the difference between you and the others," what do I say? "Well that's easy. The people. You will kayak, see the mangroves, explore the mangrove creeks, see sea life, and learn about the area, but at Lazy Dog, it's the staff that makes the difference. We love and appreciate our customers. It's more than a job."

"Be remarkable by doing more than is expected."

The SCoop

We're not in high school anymore; now, we want people talking about us!

Remember back in high school when you *didn't* want people talking about you? Well, now you do… or at least, in business you do; it's called word of mouth. You want to be so remarkable that people talk about you, share their stories about you, and tell *everyone* they know. It's one of the best ways to organically build a business.

If you want to make money, sell to your customer. If you want to build a business, build a strong customer base. A strong customer base is loyal. Such customers will seek you out, return to you time and time again and talk about you to others organically, thus giving you repeat business and word of mouth marketing. To build this kind of customer connection and loyalty, you must go beyond customer service to include, at the highest level possible, customer satisfaction.

At Lazy Dog, the focus has never been on selling; it has always been about the experiences of our customers because the goal was and still is to *build a business*, not merely make a sale. Ways we have achieved this include:

1) **Listening to what the customer wants.** By listening to our existing and potential customers, we have been able to get direct access to and learn about what people wanted, which means we were able to expand in many unforeseen areas. We grew faster and gained more trust just by listening and adjusting our plan to give customers what they needed/ desired.

2) **Creating a memorable experience.** By creating a memorable experience, we are doing much more than simply providing a service or product; we are making personal connections. When I read our TripAdvisor reviews, I realize that it is the entire *experience* that makes Lazy Dog Adventures the "highlight of their trip" for our guests because they always mention the staff, the person they spoke to over the phone, the shuttle van, and the shack, as well as their kayak tour or paddle board rental. We can always learn from a bad review, but be sure to read the great ones, too, to see what stands out, the patterns that exist, and notice carefully what matters most to your customers. Make that your focus!

3) **Offering value.** Give more to the customer than they think they're paying for—value, value, value. Share tips and recommend other activities, services, or products

you personally enjoy to create an authentic rapport and exchange stories or experiences.

Listen-Connect-Engage-Share

Listening, connecting, engaging, and sharing serve as the backbone of customer satisfaction. If you don't have enough time to spend with the most important part of your business—the people, the reason you have a business in the first place—then you're wasting your time. Take the time to connect with people. If it was their first time paddling, check back in with them and ask questions. Become part of their memorable experience. Our business is so much more than what we "sell."

Remember, your product is the people. Focus on the people.

I'm so invested in this formula that I actually have an extra employee come in during our busy hours so that my staff has the time, and knows it is okay to take time, to talk with a customer. I let them know that listen-connect-engage-share is just as important a part of the job as making a sale. I can look out and see a staff member sitting at the picnic table talking to a customer after their paddle board experience and know that is where our work has meaning. It is the most essential part of what we do!

DO THIS:

Build your customer satisfaction.

1) If you have a TripAdvisor, Facebook, Google business listing, or Instagram page, read through what people like about your business. This list will help give you a customer's viewpoint on what matters most.

2) Write down what "extra value" you can provide to your customers. If you get stuck, think about some places that you frequent where you feel you get "more than you paid for."

3) Try your customer service plan of listen-connect-engage-share yourself and see the benefits.

"I've learned that people will forget what you said, people will forget what you did, but people will never forget how you made them feel."—Maya Angelou.

Chapter 12

THE CUSTOMER IS ALWAYS RIGHT BUT NEVER FIRST

"If you don't take care of yourself first, then how are you going to take care of a customer?"

You, your staff, your customer. In that order.

Yes, we have all heard that the customer is always right, but that doesn't mean they come first. If you want to be successful in anything, you have to take care of yourself first. I've touched on this a few times already, but I can't stress it enough. What will it take to get you in peak performance physically and emotionally, every day? To bring the 100% version of yourself, every day?

If you bring less than 100%, then you are hampering your work, your relationships, and everything else. You have the power to bring it; why wouldn't you?

After taking care of you, you have what it takes to bring it to the staff. Your staff is the next most important. Take care of everything they need so that they can do the best possible job they can. Provide resources and give them support.

Next, take care of your customers. Huh? Customers come *third*? Yes, because if you don't bring your best to provide the best platform for your staff to work, then your customers will not have a good experience.

At the core of this book and each section is *you first*. When it comes to customer service, this is no different. It comes back to the old saying that if you don't take care of yourself, then you can't take care of others. How?

Take at least an hour a day to get yourself in a peak physical and emotional state. By doing this, you will then have (nearly) unlimited personal resources to give to others. You can't run out of "giving" when you fill your personal reserves.

The SCoop

Every experience starts with you.

I had an experience at a new water park that followed the philosophy of "customer first." They wanted to reduce the wait time for their water park rides. They came up with a unique concept but spent so much time focusing on the customer experience, they forgot about their staff. Every ride I went on, I asked the staff, "How's the ride?" All of them responded, "I don't know; I've never experienced it." They went on to say they were told a lot of things they would be able to do but never happened. They said the job wasn't what they were told. It led to such a negative vibe with us, the customer. The rides were great, but the overall experience was not. And exceptional businesses these days are the ones that focus on the overall experience. This starts with *you first*.

Lazy Dog on Customer Service

Customer service is a much-talked-about element of business, and I am going to give you the best advice you could receive on improving your customer service. The product or service you are selling is not your business—people are your business. That's right; put your focus on the people, and you will immediately improve your customer service. I am always aware of customer service when I'm out shopping around, and one blanket issue I see is that people are so busy doing their jobs that they forget about the people. From the grocery store bagger who handed me my bags without even looking at me to the veterinary office that was so busy behind the desk that the staff couldn't acknowledge me. You spend a lot of money trying to get your customers to call you or come in, so when they do, drop everything and be the best you you can be. There are a lot of ways to make your company more efficient, but when it comes to your customers, keep it personal. A customer plan is more important than a business plan.

Don't look at your customers as if you only want to make the sale. It's not about monetizing your customers; it's about getting them to come back. To do that, you have to help your customers rather than try to sell to your customers. You have to make them feel good. That's how you *build* a company. By the way, this can be said for building friendships and business relationships as well. People want to spend time with you or your business with people who make them feel good.

I have listed a few Lazy Dog customer service philosophies for you to try.

The answer is "Yes," then find a way to make it happen. Try to make things happen for your customer, even if it's not what you usually do. Trying will feel like a "Yes" to a customer. They will leave feeling good about your company.

Be yourself, your best self. We all get our bad days, but at work, it's like a Broadway show. Put it on, and it will help you feel better. Customers don't want to see your Off Broadway show.

Treat customers as friends. There is a big difference between forced and natural customer service. Typically, if you don't like what you're doing, you will come across forced. Try to treat customers like you would like to be treated. Imagine they are your best friend's mom and dad; doing so will change the kindness and patience level, and it will also change your tone. You will seem more organic in your interaction. For a customer to feel like they were taken care of like a friend usually will lead to a happier customer.

Give the gift. You are in a unique position to make someone's day, to be the highlight of their day, so be responsible with this gift. It could be being kind or delivering an amazing adventure or sharing a story or listening or giving someone your attention. Giving is a beautiful thing, for your customers and for you.

Give more than expected. Do more than what's expected. Give something of extra value that the customers don't think they are paying for; this makes them feel that their money was well spent.

Say "you're welcome." It always feels good when someone accepts or acknowledges your "thank you." It's as good as looking someone in the eye and acknowledging them.

Connect. Make it personal with people and what they share with you. Create an emotional connection. Follow up so that they know you were listening and care. Pay extra attention and connect to the problem customers or the customers who can make a big impact, such as those who have never been on the water before. People will always remember their first time.

Beginning, middle, end. Complete your conversation with your customers. Always be the first to offer a greeting. Stop all workplace conversations and jobs and make the customer the priority. Relay all information to the customer that's needed. The conversation doesn't end after you receive payment. Continue the connection. In my personal shopping experience, too many customer interactions fall short, with no greeting or thank you or a lack of information shared.

Be patient. Customers are coming into your place; they will be out of their zone, so be patient. It's your comfort zone, not theirs, so if they ask ridiculous questions, just go with it. Be kind and make them feel comfortable.

Listen. People love to talk about themselves. It makes them feel good. Let people talk; they will walk away feeling good about you and your business. The more you can switch the conversation to the other person, the more likely that person will come away from your company feeling good. People feel good when others listen to them.

Smile. Enjoy what you do; don't take everything so seriously.

Make it as easy as possible for people to have a good experience. Also, make it easy for them to give you money. Take all forms of payment. Yes, it costs more money to take American Express, but if that's how a customer wants to pay, let them.

Keep paperwork simple so that you spend more time with customers. People want to connect with a brand or people. Connection will lead to sales. The best way to connect with people is to spend more time talking to people and less time with paperwork and red tape.

Help customers even if it's something you don't offer. This may keep a potential customer for life. Selling to customers only gives you a sale; helping a customer gives you a repeat customer.

Be there. Make sure you as owner are there, with no other job to do but help and interact. Add an extra employee so that staff can interact with customers and not get so tied down with their job. This is where you connect, help, and make a customer for life. People are your best investment.

Don't get caught up in your job. I've been shopping many places where the customer service staff is too busy doing things that they can't help customers, or the staff is so busy stocking shelves, etc. that they get in your way when you shop.

Great customer service is a way of life. This is true not just for your customers but also for your friends, employees, vendors—everyone.

There's always one. When I was younger, my mom would say you can't please everyone (though she certainly would try). This holds true in business as well. Some people clearly just can't be happy. I've seen people who are on vacation come up to our shack to kayak, and they are absolutely miserable. They complain about everything before they even go out. Remember, there will always be people out there who we can't make happy because they won't allow it for themselves. Give some allowance and don't let it change who and what you are and how you do things.

DO THIS:

Take the time to observe people in their workplace.

When you're shopping or at a restaurant, what is it that works for you and what doesn't work? Create your own customer service plan. Try to see your business from a customer's point of view.

How do you want your customers to feel, from their first encounter to the end?

....

....

What's important to you in customer service?

....

....

As a consumer/shopper what is it that makes you feel you received good customer service?

What places that you shop make you feel that you received good customer service?

What did these places do that made you feel you received good customer service?

What do you like or how do you like to be treated?

What don't you like?

What makes an experience a great experience?

Put together this list and create a customer service plan. You can even involve your staff by having them answer these questions. Getting the staff involved will increase the chances of your customer service plan working. Your staff will also gain a heightened awareness of the customer experience.

Chapter 13

LEAD THE WAY FOR YOUR COMPETITION

"If you're doing something right, then you will have competition."

First, you are most likely your own biggest competitor. How? By getting in your own way, taking yourself out of the game too early, and telling yourself negative talk. You must get past this to be successful. The best way to do this is through action.

Now, on to the other competition. If you're doing something right, you will have competition. Congratulations! I hear people waste a lot of time talking and stress about their competitors, but if you don't have any competitors, then you probably have a struggling business. If you have competition and don't like it, you have to get over it. If you're doing something good and don't have any competition, know that you will soon. Accept it; it shows you are on a good path.

Here's the Lazy Dog philosophy on competition.

Be a pioneer. Blaze the trail. Keep thinking of what else you can do to add value and expand. Even if you weren't the first to create a certain type of business, you can be the first to add a certain element to it.

Competition isn't personal. It's usually the weak or the egocentric who make it personal. That's not you!

Stay motivated. Use competition to light a fire under you and then, keep it burning. Competition can be a good reminder not to get stagnant and too comfortable.

Keep a positive attitude. No one (staff, customers, friends) likes negative attitudes. Keep positive, and all you will see is more positive. Never put your competition down. That's for them to do, not you.

Lead the way for your competitors. If you lead, you will always be one step ahead of your competition. This is accomplished by always growing yourself, applying and being authentic.

Be unique. No one is you, so be the best you. Other people can imitate you, but they are not you. You will be on top if you stay true to who you are. Those who are trying to be you will be inauthentic, and customers will see it. If you have a similar product or service as some competition, then make what you offer different with your staff and customer service.

Know what your competitors are doing but don't focus too much on them. There is always lots to do, so don't waste your time focusing on your competition.

If they copy you, it is a compliment. Be proud of your ideas; you created them first.

See the positive in everything before you see the negative. Don't spend time complaining.

The face of small businesses is you. So, be a better person, and it will reflect on your business and your staff. No one can be a better you than you.

Grow. Keep creating. Keep dreaming. Keep believing. Read, study, talk to people, keep current, apply what you learn, and growth will come your way. Many companies become content with their success and start to stagnate. Be different. Keep growing yourself and your business.

Work within your means. Keep extra money around for the slow times. You never want to make decisions based on lack of money.

When the economy is slow or is in its low season, businesses tend to cut back, especially on marketing. If you work and spend within your means throughout the year, this will give you an opportunity to make a splash and get ahead. Some of the best companies came out of the weakest economical times because they didn't cut back on marketing.

Be open. Keep a positive mental and physical mindset to everything so that you can see what to do next. Be one step ahead of your competition.

Do things your competition can't or chooses not to do.

Always **be better at customer service.** If the products are equal, then be better with better customer service.

The SCoop

People are the focus, not profits.

One of the greatest compliments I've received over the years regarding business was when someone introduced themselves and said I changed the way companies do business in Key West because I focused on the people.

Of course, all businesses want to make money, but if that is your main focus, then you can't help but lose sight of people. Focusing on money means focusing on making a sale, but focusing on people (you, your staff, your customers) builds a business, and that's how we build Lazy Dog. It means the profits will come later on down the road, but they will come.

First or Last, Find Your Niche

If you're first in the market, then following the preceding tips will help keep you there. Focus on the *what* and the *why* you are doing, and, most importantly, don't get stagnant.

If you are entering an already established market, find a niche within that market that the others aren't taking advantage of and then, lead the way.

When I started out, there were other kayak companies around, but they seriously lacked any customer service. They were downright awful. This is why I was able to find legs quickly and grow. Lazy Dog was the first to come in with paddle board rentals and tours, so if a company wants to come in and find their way, they should look at the areas where we are not doing something. For example, someone might want to make night tours their signature and grow their business out from there. Your business can overlap with others, but find your niche to stand out.

DO THIS:
Keep moving forward ahead of the competition.

What is unique about you (your business)?
What can you do that your competition doesn't do?
What do you do great? Keep doing them.
What could you do better? Do it!
What can you say about your competition that you can't say about yourself?
What can your competition say about you that they can't say about themselves?

Chapter 14

HOSTING EVENTS & CREATING EXPERIENCES

"If it leads to more fun then the answer is yes."

I've always enjoyed hosting parties of all kinds—theme parties, dress-up parties, you name it. So, it came naturally for me when I ventured into hosting events. Hosting events isn't for everyone. They are stressful and never go according to plan. I used to have to remind my staff of this at each event. I told them that not even Madonna's multi-million-dollar concerts go off without a hitch. It's okay; it's all in how we handle it.

There's a great energy around events that I like. In a way, it's like creating a small business that runs for a day, hopefully successfully. I love the energy that surrounds events.

I like to think that my expertise in running events comes from hosting and attending events. Like parties, I love events: paddle races, running races, festivals, expos. I've traveled around the country to attend events because I love participating in fun. I have become aware of what works and what doesn't, and my always-working business mind sees the gaps and wants to fill or fix things. So, when it came time for me to create an event, I used what I thought worked and built from there.

The SCoop

Learn from others, but make each event your own.

I particularly remember a paddle race in Puerto Rico. We got on a boat and sailed out to sea for 8 miles, whereupon the crew threw our paddle boards overboard. We jumped in the water and had to race back to Puerto Rico. It was so much fun. I found myself saying I wish we had something like this in Key West. Instead of listening to myself complain how I wished this race was in Key West, I decided to create it. Remember, Lazy Dog's motto #1 is, *If it doesn't exist, create it!* There is now an annual race hosted by Lazy Dog called Race the Reef. We hire a sailboat to take everyone out to the reef, about 6 miles out, and throw the boards over. Everyone jumps off and races back to Key West.

Events cost money to run, but our focus is always on fun (after safety). Events aren't about making money, but I certainly don't want to lose money. From a business perspective, events are great organic marketing tools. We create and provide a platform where people can have an experience that they might not have had otherwise. Seeing them complete their goal or participate in the experience is a thrill like no other for me and my crew. By providing a safe, fun event, people can have an experience that they will share and talk about for a long time (word-of-mouth advertising).

The last seven years, we have created four annual events around paddle boarding. Before the events existed, I participated in paddle board races around the country. This gave me hands-on experience. For example, after months of training and then waking up on race day, the last thing I want to do is wait in a long line for registration. This is a common problem at events, but it's an easy fix: no day-of registration. Have people register the night before, during a 2-hour window during happy hour, keeping it light, social, and with plenty of time to complete the process. The next day, you can free up people at check-in, which is where most of the questions and issues arise. Providing race numbers the day before is another easy fix, but definitely have more people at check-in than you need. Through my experiences, we were able to put on events that worked not only for us the organizers but, most importantly, for the participants. It's about having fun, and if you can do that for the participants, then it will be a successful event.

The SCoop

Keep these in mind.

Whether it's hosting a paddle board race, seminar, workshop, or class, I have a few general guidelines that we follow:

1. If the answer leads to more fun, then the answer is "yes." Recently, we were hosting a paddle board race and some racers asked if we could reverse the race course. We said "yes," and they were so excited and pumped up. It created a buzz as everyone started talking about it. *Yes!* It made it more fun.

2. Be as cool as a cucumber. The vibe of your event will come from you. If you are stressed and running around panicking, people will pick up on your negative energy.

3. Your event is more than just an event; it's an experience. The entire experience lasts through sign-up, pre-event, event, timing, awards, post-event, and follow up, so pay attention to it all and finish strong.

4. It won't go off without a hitch, so adjust as you go and keep a great attitude.

The SCoop

Give more value.

As I said, events don't always bring in a lot of money, leading people to cancel them before they start or to not continue hosting. I see events more as a marketing tool, but there are many side opportunities around all events. Here's a way to bring value to your event:

Invite top talent to give clinics. In the case of paddle boarding, these professional athletes want to make money, and you are the platform. Reach out to them and make it as easy as possible for them to come down and make money by sharing their knowledge. You, in turn, increase your value with top talent. While working with top talent, part of our arrangement is to cross-promote. Lazy Dog promotes the clinic, but we ask that the talent promote the clinic at Lazy Dog to their followers.

Say, for example, you are a personal trainer and want to get a specific certification, but all the workshop classes are far away and cost a lot of money. Reach out to the certified trainer and ask them to come to you. You promote their event for others to pay and attend, and you get to go for free. This puts your personal training business in the forefront of hosting certifications and top talent, setting you apart. Make it worth their while. You are the business person, and you are dealing with athletes, so help them help themselves. Helping them out helps you.

Being in Key West, we are far away and not necessarily an economical destination for athletes, so we make it economical by setting them up with a schedule: our event, plus maybe one up the Keys and another in Miami. Do the work and make it easy for the talent, and they will be back

Again, events are so much more than just that, but that's where the energy tends to go. I like to look at the big picture. Here's an example from our Key West Paddle around the Island race. It's more than simply the entry fee that matters. The preparation, not only for you but for your participants, is part of the buildup and the payoff.

1) Throughout the year, every Tuesday, we host paddle training for beginners to experienced paddlers.
2) We sell products, such as paddles and gear.
3) Paddlers bring their friends out on other days.
4) We gain exposure, every time someone comes out to train.

5) We partner with clinics.
6) We gain organic marketing posts.
7) Word-of-mouth advertising means people talking about us.
8) It also builds our customer base.
9) We stand out in the paddle racing community.
10) We receive free national advertising by listing our race.

So, even if you just break even, you can still run a successful event.

Chapter 15

OFF THE LEASH MARKETING & SALES

"Do the things the way you want to do them, not the way you have been told."

Marketing is one of my favorite parts of our Lazy Dog business, and I think it's because we really only market what we truly believe in. It's 100% *organic*, and that's because of our company culture. By doing what we love and making that so clearly visible to all who see Lazy Dog, we attract others with similar "culture" to join. This makes business become much more like a lifestyle for all.

When tapping into your passion and what you organically love, creativity bursts out of the seams, flowing freely. Everything becomes easier, things seem to make sense, and the puzzle pieces come together.

Marketing, The Lazy Dog Way

Do things! Market your company through what you do in your personal life. Have fun with your free time (attending events, races, parties). What you do for fun shapes your business. Embrace it! Become an extension of your brand. Always remember the value of authenticity. What you do for fun also shapes your business *reputation*, so get involved and live your mission statement. Richard Branson from Virgin Air did this best. He hosted all kinds of events and stunts (hot air ballooning around the world, for example), and he saw his personal visibility and that of his companies boom.

Be different. Do things differently even if it's only slightly different. Doing the same as everyone else will make you the same as everyone else, and if you are in business, I know you don't want to be like everyone else. You want to stand out.

Market to *every* group. Old, new, seasonal, late-night, early-morning, snowbirds, high-income, artists, athletes, and politicians. Don't market to your crowd or the crowd you are comfortable in only. Sometimes, marketing yourself to a group that's not your target makes a bigger splash.

Create stories. Social media sites, magazines, and blogs want you! Create a fun event or a story, and then, get the press to follow. it You're giving the media what they want, which is a story. That's right, you are making it as easy as possible for them to do their job. Create a story around your business to get more media attention. Creating interesting stories and events is easy, especially the more you do it. Make giving you press easy for the media by providing the story or event, quotes, and great high-quality photos.

The SCoop

Create a story.

About 15 years ago, one of the Lazy Dog employees had her dog Bonny stolen from the marina while we were all at work there. We got the guy on surveillance video, but he drove home to Miami with the dog, and we had no idea who he was. The story was on the front page of the local newspapers and made it into *The Miami Herald* and on the Miami TV news stations. Everyone was talking about it, but after two weeks, there was still no word. I asked *The Miami Herald* to rerun the story, but the reporter told me it was an old story. She told me to create something else, and she would write about that. So, I hired a plane in Miami to tow a banner up Miami Beach and over all the sporting events that read, "Where Is Bonny.com Reward!" I was lucky enough to find a plane service in Miami owned by a dog lover. He gave me a deal on the banner and then contacted all the local newspapers and TV outlets in Miami and told them the story. He said that he was going to fly the plane around and tow the banner. He told the media outlets his exact flying route and times and flew over the TV stations so that they could film it. It was a fresh approach to an old story, and all media picked it up. We got a call that day from a friend of the guy who had stolen the dog; he was going to return the dog to us. It was a tough 17 days, and we all aged a lot during that time, but I learned some valuable lessons about working with the media.

Make or create the marketing tools that people who can promote you want. Remember, make it as easy as possible for customers to find (then buy) your product or service. If a restaurant server asks for business cards to give out to customers, but all you have are brochures, make cards for them. They're cheap and effective. If you have someone doing your marketing, give them all the tools they need to do their job. If you don't, you are wasting their time and your money.

Give back to your community.. This is great for company bonding. Make a difference, and do it as a company. Give to your community. The good you do always comes back to you. This is the most rewarding part of business, and if you don't have money, then time is just as valuable. Becoming a member of your community solidifies you and your business within your town.

Say "thank you." After a customer has experienced your business, send a thank you of some kind. This could be a post on their social media, an email, or even a postcard thanking them for their business. Make the "thank you" fun and exciting so that they will talk about it.

Be an expert at something. Post on social media, blog, write, and share what you have. Share your knowledge and have your staff contribute too. People want to learn, so share what you know. People will follow content, but don't try to sell them something. Eventually, if they like what you share, they will find out what else you do, and that is when you can sell your products.

Use the platforms that exist. Content is king. People, websites, and social media sites are always looking for good content, and you can provide free content. Find what they are looking for, relate it to your business, create the content, and send it in.

Create memorable experiences for others. Events are one of my favorite and most fun and rewarding marketing tools. There is nothing better than creating a platform for people to have a great time. Do something, especially if it's for their first time. When people do something for the first time, there is added energy to the event for them. It makes a lasting impression and is great post-marketing. Events are such great, organic marketing tools because people who participate in your events become marketers for your business and your events by telling and retelling their experiences.

Handle post-event marketing. Marketing isn't over when the event happens. Post-marketing is just as important. Continue all marketing efforts after the event to keep your event in the spotlight longer. Keep people talking about it. Sign them up now for the next event, share testimonials, and share pictures. Be the official photographer; take pictures of *everyone* and let people know your website or Facebook page is the place to see all those pictures.

Cross-market. I love working with interesting people, and there have been many times when we have cross-marketed with another company so that I could work with someone I like and admire. It opens up creativity when you work with new people outside your business.

Find ways outside your company to bring attention to your company by indirect marketing. You can do this through public speaking, writing a blog, posting YouTube videos, writing a book, being on the board of a charity group, hosting events, and more.

The SCoop

Use every angle to promote.

The best example to explain this is in the marketing of my first book, which included stories from my college, the University of Massachusetts at Amherst, my adventures in Kauai and Key West, numerous paddle board races, and top racing talent. When it came time to market my book, I used all these angles. For Key West, I had small stickers made to put on the cover of the book that said, "Local author and business owner." For Kauai, I created a sticker that said, "Includes local Kauai stories." For UMASS, I called the alumni office and shared my book with them. They featured my book in the alumni magazine. For the races, I tag them all in social media. Get creative and find organic links in what you do relating to other people, places, and things. These days, this is so much easier with social media.

If you build it, they will come. Don't wait for things to happen. For example, make your own video commercials or write a book and produce it yourself. You don't need to pay someone to create, produce, and show your commercial or book or whatever you want to put out there. Make what you need happen. Don't rely on others.

We have done some ridiculously silly things over the years and gained a lot of press by being silly and just trying things out. There are no real rules here. It's kind of an anything-goes, no-structure marketing. Once you get into creative marketing and all you can do, you will start to see things from multiple angles. It gets fun.

Growing up, I always liked the word "creative." I took that word as a compliment. The problem was that I was never called creative. It wasn't until I followed my passion that it happened for me. Everything suddenly became clear, and even though I didn't know what I was doing, I was doing what I loved. I let go of all the things I didn't like and all the things that didn't work for me, and I entered a creative space. I saw the direction I wanted to go, and I had the space now that the crap was gone to be creative. New things I had never seen before came into my life. I *am* creative! Even if I'm the only one who tells me so.

Think Outside the Box

There is no box. When I was interviewing at Adidas, they had painted this crazy, big-wheel oversized truck. They did it because it was their roaming billboard. They would drive it to national events that were too expensive to advertise at and park it; these were places such as the Super Bowl and World Series. Make it fun so that people want to take a picture next to it. One of my favorite examples is a local plumber who designed his truck so that there's an image of a toilet seat under the window of the driver's side door; when he's driving, he looks like he's sitting on the toilet. Everyone photographs it, posts it, and he sticks out in our minds when we need a plumber.

We needed storage for our shirts, so instead of renting warehouse space, we purchased a 21-foot enclosed trailer and wrapped it with our logo. The trailer can be taken to events, but most of the time, it faces the main highway in our parking lot and serves as a billboard.

We contacted the University of Texas at Austin's advertising department to ask if they would use our company as their guinea pig for class. The class was broken down into five groups of five; they had to create their own advertising company and then use us as a client. Each group interviewed me on the phone and then came up with an advertising campaign that they presented to us. It was pretty incredible and provided us with great ideas to help grow our brand.

The best way to think outside the box is to think big! If money and resources are no object, then see what you can realistically do.

When I worked in the corporate world, we would spend $80,000 on a 2-page spread ad in a high-end fashion magazine (not to mention all the money and time we spend picking out models, the photo shoot, and so on). I personally thought it was a waste of money. I understand that magazines have to make money, but for our shoe company brand and where we were, it was a waste of money. My strong reaction to the waste of money was my first eye-opener to the fact that maybe I was better suited to be an entrepreneur (and not a corporate employee). Oh, the things I could do to market, promote, and get our shoe brand out there for $80,000! I could get more visibility and probably make it last a year rather than blow $80,000 a month. I cared too much about that ad; I felt it was a waste. I was meant to be an entrepreneur.

Entrepreneurs like to do things differently, and I think my experience with the magazine ad fueled my desire never to spend money on print advertising. I used this as a rule of thumb when I first started out, and it forced me to be more creative with marketing.

Start local. If there is something that you want to do on a big scale, nationally or globally such as sell a product, become a keynote speaker, or create a global charity, but you don't have the means or funds to do so, then the next best thing to do is to start smaller in your community. Community is the best place to build anything. Don't get discouraged by not having resources to do what you want on a big scale; just start where you are, and you will be surprised.

Give it away. When people call and ask for donations, I have a rule. We provide free rental cards, which has a $100 value, that can be used for raffles or auctions. We do this because if we donated cash to everyone that asked for a donation, we would be broke. There are so many events and fundraisers, so instead of having to pick a few to donate cash to, we provide the rental cards and can donate to all. We only support local Key West, but we help all that ask. When people come up to us an ask for a donation we say "Absolutely," give them a card, and then always say, "Thank you for including us." Saying "thank you" always stumps the person asking.

It's never easy to ask for something for free, but we appreciate that people come to us, appreciate us, and ask, so we thank them. I don't think they hear "thank you" very often when they are asking for donations.

The SCoop

Opportunities are everywhere, especially the ones we don't know about.

I decided when I wrote my first book that my primary customer was looking for that laid-back Key West lifestyle. So, I put my marketing efforts into Key West and grew it from there. I used a few thousand dollars and bought my own books; then, my marketing manager, Barb, took them to the guest houses with which we already had great relationships and asked if they would put my book in their guest rooms as a complimentary room copy. Almost every single guest house Barb went to was excited about the idea. In a matter of two weeks, she had my book in over 620 guest house rooms. Do you know how much money it usually costs to get an ad in an in-room magazine? It was the best couple thousand dollars I've spent. I thought of it not only as a way for people to enjoy my book (and hopefully buy their own copy), but that maybe while they were on vacation, they would want to visit Lazy Dog and see what it's all about. Or maybe they would want to meet Casey dog or me. Our business *boomed*. But what happened next was a complete surprise.

Billionaires and Scientists
Have you ever heard of The Explorer's Club? I hadn't. It's a worldwide organization of a bunch of billionaires who fund scientists to explore all around the world. One of the chapter presidents of the Explorer's Club, who was staying in a guest house in Key West, happened upon my book in his room while he was on vacation. The next thing I know, I'm being asked to be in The Explorer's Club.

After my manager, Kathy, told me about the club, I told the president, "I'm not a billionaire or a scientist." He said he read my book, and he wanted more people with my energy and vision in the club to give it a spark. Oh, I can do *that!* I joined after a lengthy process of being vetted; most of the questions I had to answer were non-applicable, but I was officially invited as a member. For fun, I decided to go to their annual meeting where some big name scientists, billionaires, and celebrities attend and you get to eat cow testicles, scorpions, and ants, among other things. I invited my besties Holly and Sandy, and we got ourselves all dolled up with fancy hairdos and formal dresses and flew to New York. It was a fun experience, and we met some amazing people. I have always wanted to organize a "research" trip with the Explorer's Club, but I have yet to do it. So much to do. This story always reminds me that there is so much we don't know but that by aligning ourselves with people, places, and experiences, great things present themselves. You simply need to keep and open mind and be ready.

Social Media Marketing

"If you're not on social media, it doesn't mean you won't be successful, but you won't be as successful as you could be."

I don't want to spend too much time here talking social media since it changes every millisecond, but I will share a few basics for using social media to build your business and leave you with an incredible resource to keep on top of the ever-changing world of social.

First, if you are not doing social media, then you are making things very hard on yourself. You won't be as successful as you could be.

I know it can be overwhelming. I hear you; you don't have the time, right? So, you're telling me that you don't have the time to reach directly to your customer's phone, for free. If you have a café, you don't have the time to post your daily specials? You don't have time to reach right to where your customers, attention is?

Don't get lost. People get lost in scrolling, checking out what other people are doing, and in seeing how many likes they've received on a post.

Here's what you should be doing: 80% of your time on social media should be commenting on and liking other posts. Don't worry about *your* "likes;" that's ego. Comment and engage with others, and they will start to follow you.

The SCoop

Social media is the single biggest, high-reward, low-cost marketing plan out there. So, why wouldn't you?

Engaging with followers is easy. One simple and effective way we have done this is to include the followers in our decisions we make at Lazy Dog, to be part of the process. For example, we have picked a new shirt design but can't decide what colors to print. Asking our customers to vote brings engagement.

We've talked a lot in this book about changing your perspective and your mindset. This is a must-do for social media.

- Don't look at it as something else you have to do. Look at it as the greatest advertising opportunity you could possibly imagine, to reach millions of people for free.

- Do it yourself; don't hire it out. This is most important. Your brand is an extension of you.
- Just like you schedule the time to work out, schedule time each day for social media.
- Social media is free—*use* it!

There are so many platforms that exist within social media that are looking for content. Provide them with pictures, articles, and content.

Here's your social media briefing.

- The overall idea with social media is to connect with your customers. Don't use social media to sell to your customers. You want to use social media to CONNECT EMOTIONALLY. Make it easy for people to have an emotional moment.
- Make it PERSONAL, not an ad. Be and show VULNERABILITY.
- Be UNIQUE.
- This is what you do for a living; you are an EXPERT in this. Be the EXPERT. People will follow you. Share a tip of the day or include quotes.
- Be of VALUE. What can you provide so that they want to follow and come back to you?
- Present in a short and interesting manner.
- People want information, so share what you have. Post behind-the-scenes content (and remember it's good to be vulnerable).
- Be consistent about posting.
- Post, comment, like, and share.
- Find your niche and be the expert.
- HASHTAG everything on Instagram; it will help more people see your post.
- It's not merely posting but engaging with followers and following other people that's important.
- Watch engagement. See what people like and what gets shared.

Here are a few things to consider in your social media plan.

- Be on it all; all these sites are *free!* Facebook, Instagram, YouTube, Twitter, LinkedIn
- Each site has a different purpose, so don't post the same content on each; mix it up.
- Use pictures, short videos, storytelling, reviews, how-tos, and questions.

Some questions to ask yourself are:

- What can you provide to followers that will make them come back?
- What are you doing that makes you unique?
- What are you doing that's different from anyone else?

How best to use your social media changes daily. For the most up-to-date and off-the-wall social media plans, check out Gary Vaynerchuk on YouTube.

DO THIS:
Engage

This is a social media growth plan from my favorite Gary Vaynerchuck video for Instagram. It's his $1.80 program.

1) Find 9 hashtags that are relevant to you.
2) Take the top 10 most popular posts within those hashtags and leave a comment.
3) Be sure your comment is something of value, not just an emoji.
4) That's 9 hashtags with 10 comments each, which equal 90 comments with your two cents for a total of $1.80.

I know this might take you a while in the beginning, but remember this is the cheapest marketing campaign EVER.

Sales, the Lazy Dog Way

I'm not the greatest at sales because I tend to "give the farm away." I get excited when people come out, and if they are nice, I give things away at a discount. I don't know why I do this, but at least I know I do, so I pull in people when needed to handle the money. My best friend Holly (the "Songwriter" for the band), who is also our product manager, is the "shark." She does the negotiating when it comes to our events. Kathy handles most of the financial things for Lazy Dog, and she can be a shark too. I know my weaknesses, and I counter them with people who are strong. It's a team effort. I have a few basic rules for selling and being sold to.

1) Make it as easy as possible for someone to do business with you. For example, take all forms of payment, have a simple sign-in system, allow people to sign documents online, have items in stock, deliver…

2) People will buy from you if they like you. Be nice. Relate.

3) Understand what people are looking for and give them what they need.

4) Sell the outcome. Sales isn't about you; it's about what you can give of value to the end user. I like Sara Blakely's story of when she sold Spanx to a buyer at Neiman Marcus. She didn't go in with an attitude that the sale was for her, or even for the buyer. She sold Spanx by saying this product will change the way customers feel in their clothing.

5) Don't focus on the sale only, or you will never build a business. Focus on the people. Connect, engage, listen, and share. Build relationships.

6) Numerous people have tried to sell me products in such a technical manner that they lose me. The salesperson is caught up on the features rather than presenting it as a product that makes sense for me and my customers.

7) Don't answer for someone. Don't think that you know how someone will answer. Say what you want and let the chips fall. I have spent way too much time on this consulting with businesses. I waste my time trying to convince business owners to stop answering for their clients and customers. Just put it out there and see what happens.

I remember working on a project, and we wanted to present it to the cruise ships. I was told by others who worked with the cruise lines that they wouldn't be interested, and they told me all the reasons why. We could have stopped there, but I didn't want to be the reason the ships said no. Let them tell me. So, we presented our proposal of how it could be more than just a local excursion but one they could use in all their ports. The cruise line agreed to our proposal. We didn't listen to other people's advice and went ahead anyway and presented our idea. The answer is no… unless you ask.

Our proposal was no different than any other proposal, which is to sell the buyer something that will give their customer an incredible experience. Where we could have gone wrong was listening to other people who considered themselves "experts" with the cruise ships. Don't ever take yourself out of the game before it even starts.

My friend has a business in Key West, and I advised her to set up an online store. She said it would be too expensive to ship and that people wouldn't pay for it. I told her if I wanted a lobster from Maine, I would pay to have it shipped overnight. If someone wants your unique product, and Key West is the only place to get it, people will pay for shipping. She was answering "no" for the customer before even giving it a try. She eventually tested the online market and, what do you know, people had no problem paying the overnight shipping, which in some cases was more than the cost of the product. Don't answer for the customer. Let the customer decide yes or no.

KEEP MOVING FORWARD

Keep things interesting, keeps things fresh, and keep growing. If you keep doing the same things all the time, you won't be getting any better at *anything*.

Read, listen, and learn every day. Not everything you listen to every day will resonate with you, but with an open mind, you will find that almost every encounter and everything you listen to will have a message with something that you can implement into your day, your business, your growth.

The best lives come from a positive attitude, so keep one; it's a choice, and the alternative sucks. Be sure to keep a positive, open mind, especially when things don't work out, because that's when great opportunities present themselves.

You know that saying, "If it was easy, everyone would do it"? It will be hard, but the hard things are always so much more worth it. Don't let someone you don't even know derail you from your dream because they made a negative comment. Even the most amazing people get negative comments. There are those people out there who always see the negative and don't like anything, but they are miserable and will never experience greatness. So, let them be and keep yourself moving onward and upward.

Do your thing, live your passion, be unique and authentic, and have something to share. To be great, you need to do great things. Doing the same thing, getting the same result that you are not satisfied with, isn't going to work. Be different. Get people talking about you. Bring value, every day!

The time is now! If you don't do it, someone else will.

As kids, we are full of dreams, and it's all possible. There are ways to do whatever it is you want. If you want it bad enough, you will find a way. Excuses are for the unsuccessful. Jump in and make things happen.

The only difference between someone who is "successful" and someone who isn't is that they took action. Do something!

The 7 As of Success

Attitude – is everything.

Align – yourself with the people and things you love, and opportunities will come your way.

Awareness – is one of the most important traits you can have. Find it!

Action – is key; things don't change without action.

Apply – knowledge. Knowledge will only take you so far; you have to apply what you learn.

Adapt - as you go and always remember that if it doesn't work for you that it's okay to walk away.

Appreciate – everything; the two most important words to say as much as you can each day are "Thank you."

Our Mission Statement

Life is an adventure… a journey that should be met with a wide-open mind. Lazy Dog strives to create a work environment that challenges our capabilities and fuels our enthusiasm. This dynamic work environment nurtures our adventurous spirit and promotes the philosophy that our degree of success is measured only by the amount of fun we have while achieving it. The Lazy Dog brand was conceived out of affection for a single faithful pet and expresses a simple attitude that both residents and visitors alike identify with. Find your passion and make it your life's work. We at Lazy Dog believe in what we do and would like to inspire others to do the same.

More recently, we have added this daily mission:

Be the highlight of people's vacations.

Our business is simple: build and create a fun, safe, personable, and memorable experience that was more than our customers expected.

It's about experiences and opportunities, not stuff. It's about taking everything you do and adding extra value to it. We strive to take the ordinary and one-up it. Passion is our drive, not profits—but profits are the result of following our passion.

Similar to a personal mission statement, if things come up that don't match your mission statement, then lean more toward passing and keep focused on you and your company's goals.

Our Company Culture

- Our answer is "yes," then we figure out how to make it happen.
- We go into everything we do from a positive mindset. Attitude is everything.
- Everyone does everything.
- Be community driven.
  › Keep money local whenever possible.
  › Support your community (businesses, events, people).
- We are flexible, so you can adjust as you need to for situations that arise.
- We give more than is expected.
- We have pride in our product.
- By helping others, customers or staff develop loyalty and commitment.
- A slow build creates a strong foundation. Do a little something every day to grow the business.
- Limit use of the word "no."
- Be givers.
- Respect everyone.
- Take the high road.
- Be the highlight of people's vacation.
- Helping a customer leads to a customer for life.
- Take the time, make the time.
- Make people feel safe to make mistakes.
- Be the leg. Go where needed.
- Make it easy for customers to have fun with you.
- Appreciate everyone. THANK everyone.

Our Core Values

1. TEAM – Do what's needed, all hands approach. Everyone does everything.
2. POSITIVE ATTITUDE – Attitude is everything.
3. HELP EVERYONE – management, staff, neighboring businesses, our customers, others' customers.
4. TAKE CARE OF YOURSELF – so you can be your best self (flex schedules, fitness, health, travel).
5. LEARN, APPLY, GROW.
6. RESPECT EVERYONE.
7. THE ANSWER IS "YES" – then figure out how to make it happen.
8. LISTEN – this is the greatest gift you can give anyone.
9. BE THE HIGHLIGHT OF PEOPLE'S VACATIONS.
10. CONTRIBUTE LOCALLY.

ABOUT THE AUTHOR

Sue Cooper is an entrepreneur, owner of Lazy Dog Adventures in Key West, Florida, and author of the books Millionaire In Flip Flops, The Lifestyle Edition, and The Take Action Work Book.

Sue still loves going to work at Lazy Dog, growing her business, building her Lazy Dog merchandise line, and working with entrepreneurs. She travels the world with her friends, getting herself into crazy adventures, and spreading the Lazy Dog love. Her passion is to live life through having great adventures and experiences and sharing, inspiring, and empowering people to do the same. It doesn't matter how good you are at things; all that matters is that you do things. #makingmemories

She lives in Key West with her dog, Jax, a rescue border collie.

You can follow Sue Cooper at:

Sue Cooper on Facebook
@LazyDogSue on Instagram
Business website LazyDog.com
Blog at MillionaireinFlipFlops.com

Manifest Your Life

When you do the mind and body work, bring the 100% best version of yourself, be consistent, do things you are passionate about, treat people with respect, keep an open mind, and be consistent, *every day*, life and opportunities will present themselves. It's when we are in alignment with our minds and bodies every day that life starts to meet us half way.

Life Goals by Sue

Dream Big. When I was younger, I worked hard but didn't do the work to know what I really wanted. When I went to bed, I dreamed of all the possibilities.

Jump In. When I was in my 30s and early 40s, I started doing the mind and body work. It was like building a muscle, and it took time. I started jumping in and saying "yes." When I went to bed, I would say, "Wow, that was amazing. I can't believe I just did that. How fun."

Life meets you half-way. In my mid-40s, the mind and body work are part of my everyday routine. I dream big and jump in no matter if I'm good at something or not. It's all about the experiences, learning, and then sharing what I've learned. Now, when I go to bed, I say with oh so much gratitude, "Of course that just happened."

For the latest from The Adventures of Lazy Dog and Sue Cooper check out www.LazyDog and Sue's blog at www. MillionaireInFlipFlops.com

Thank you to my mentors and personal "advisors" over the years:

Veronica Cooper
Richard Cooper
Julie Cooper
Holly Amodio
Robyn Roth
Kathy Gilmour
Tim Ferris
Jesse Itzler
Tony Robbins
Gary Vaynerchek
Pat Croce
Richard Branson
Key West
The Kalalau Trail
And my Lazy Dog Staff

Made in the USA
Lexington, KY
29 November 2019